PUPPETS AND MASKS

PUPPETS AND MASKS
Stagecraft and Storytelling

NAN RUMP

DAVIS PUBLICATIONS, INC.
Worcester, Massachusetts

Dedicated to my brother George,
an excellent role model for anyone working with children

Copyright 1996
Davis Publications, Inc.
Worcester, Massachusetts U.S. A.

Cover photograph by Tim Lynch Photography

Editor: Nancy Burnett
Design and Composition: Janis Owens

Library of Congress Catalog Card Number: 94-73962

ISBN: 0-87192-298-3

Acknowledgments

Many thanks to David Dusenbury who took up the slack in all the other areas of my life, enabling me to spend untold hours in front of the computer and drawing board; to Maxie Chambliss and Susan Goodman who provided insights, expertise and constructive criticism with great sensitivity; to Bob Antia, Carol Bershad and Davis Sweet for their computer counseling; and to my children, Emma and Gabe, who often interrupted their own activities to model for the illustrations.

Special thanks to Momoko Hirose, Sharice Peters, Josh Raymond and their parents for helping with the cover photo, and to the people at Davis Publications who guided a novice through the many stages necessary to produce this book.

Contents

PART ONE

"AM I CRAZY TO TRY THIS?"

A Peek at the Possibilities

The room vibrates with accomplishment. At a nearby table, Japanese villagers are taking shape from a stack of paper plates. Slouching in the far corner, a great hulking ogre with a gap-toothed grin and stringy blue hair is receiving a manicure. Stapler in hand, you glide past the various construction sites until you are summoned to perform emergency surgery on a flamboyant paper rooster with a wandering leg. A few well-placed staples, and this gaily striped dandy struts across the desk on two sound limbs.

You are running a storytelling arts workshop for children!

Children are refreshingly unselfconscious when given the opportunity to express themselves creatively. By organizing a puppet and mask theater project, you can offer them just such an opportunity to flex their imaginations—while you wander through the developing landscapes of their fantasies and rub shoulders with the characters who live there.

To guide children through such an activity, you need only the following attributes:

- Enthusiasm
- Flexibility
- Organizational skills
- A sense of humor
- Shin guards *

*I was just kidding about the shin guards.

This book will give you the information and encouragement you need to become involved in a storytelling arts project. You don't have to be a professional puppeteer, mask maker, art teacher or drama coach. You can give children an enjoyable experience with storytelling theater even if you've never even looked a puppet squarely in the eye before.

Any reasonably sized room will do for a site. The practical information offered in this book is adaptable for any elementary school, scout troop or summer camp.

What Is a Storytelling Arts Project?

Let's say you decide to organize such a project. What is it you will be doing? First you choose a story and read it to the children who will be working on the activity. The story can be a folktale, a contemporary story, an historical narrative or an original story of the children's invention.

A few days before your project begins, you gather materials together and perform some preparatory foundation work. After setting up work areas, you are on hand to provide assistance as the children enthusiastically create puppets, masks and scenery.

The projects described in this book are designed to encourage children to experiment with dramatic communication through gesture and body language while wearing masks, manipulating puppets and moving interactive scenery. Concealing the puppeteers is not important; when the children move puppets or scenery in an evocative manner, the eyes of the audience will be drawn toward the movement. In many cases the puppeteers will be in plain view. When the children concentrate on projecting their dramatic energies through the puppets, masks and scenery, the audience will not be distracted by this openness, but will find it offers additional appeal.

Excitement builds as the grand finale approaches. The children use their creations to perform their unique interpretation of the chosen story for an invited audience of parents and peers. The children will be justly proud of their endeavors, the audience will see a captivating show, and you will feel a warm glow of accomplishment for making it all possible.

By offering this type of activity to children, you are giving them a rare exposure to all aspects of the performing arts. They do not merely watch a storyteller at work, they become the storytellers. They are the puppeteers, mask makers, scenery designers, stage hands, musicians and creative designers. This experience will nourish children's communication and social skills, and demonstrate the benefits of concentration, self-expression and cooperative effort. As children are drawn into the project, they will gain new confidence in their abilities, exercise their fertile imaginations—and have a lot of fun together!

How to Use This Book

You might use these puppet- and mask-making instructions to organize a show or parade in which children use their creative enthusiams as part of community or school fundraising efforts.

Puppets and masks can also provide a dramatic way to communicate the goals and values your community or school wishes to advocate, such as tolerance or nonviolent methods of conflict resolution.

You and the children can utilize this kind of storytelling arts project to explore the resources of your school system. An art teacher could help chil-

dren explore different design techniques, and a music teacher could lend talents in the area of sound effects, homemade musical instruments and ethnic music. A librarian could provide the children with background information and pictures.

This medium offers an ideal opportunity for studying the history of different countries and cultures. Children can become acquainted with the costumes, animals, landscapes and architecture of a particular place or people through books audiovisual materials and magazines. They can employ this information when designing the puppets, masks and scenery to dramatize a story or folktale from that country. A parent, grandparent or other community resource person could be invited in to talk about their experiences in the country being studied and to teach children a few words of the native language, which the children could then incorporate into their dramatization.

Play a recording of ethnic music from the country of study while children construct their puppets and masks. Public libraries can be a helpful resource in this area.

This type of project does not have to be an all-or-nothing effort for the person supervising it. You can share some of the preparation and organizational duties with others. This is a perfect opportunity to get parent volunteers involved in an exciting group project. Ask for their help in preparing puppet and mask foundations and in providing assistance at children's work areas.

Assure them that no experience or expertise is required.

Plan your project to fit your time schedule and inclinations. You might decide to plunge right in, in a concentrated workshop fashion. This would require that you organize a room into different work areas so that all children could work on their different puppets, masks and scenery at the same time. Group rehearsals and performances would take place shortly after construction work has been completed.

You might take a more relaxed, long-term approach and allow small groups or individuals to work on their parts of the project as time allows, storing completed creations until everyone is finished and you are ready to use them.

Or you could use this book as a simple guide for making puppets and masks to be used as creative teaching tools for introducing new ideas and curriculum material.

Children can be stimulated to develop their language skills by writing descriptions of fictional characters of their own invention, using simile and metaphor to describe physical appearances and personality traits of the characters. As a follow-up activity, each child might make a mask of the character and wear it to give a brief presentation showing how the invented character might move, gesture and interact with others.

Children could create speaking masks depicting historical figures or characters from books, then don the masks to give oral presentations, speaking as their characters and giving eyewitness descriptions of historical events or incidents from the books.

Use the puppets as teaching tools to develop motor skills and coordinated cooperative movement. Through role playing puppets can also be useful aids in exploring conflict resolution and understanding human characteristics and emotions.

The most effective way to teach children the joys and satisfaction of art is to get them directly involved in producing artworks of their own. Every child can produce interesting and unique artistic creations if provided with the opportunity, the encouragement and the motivation. Every child deserves a chance to experience the pleasures to be found in such a creative outlet.

The puppet and mask construction instructions (Chapters 2 through 4) are organized into two sections:

"Paving the Way" describes preparatory work usually undertaken by an adult.

"Children's Activity" discusses steps children take to develop and complete their puppets and masks.

Children can construct their creations from scratch if you prefer. *For safety sake, however, any steps requiring the use of a utility knife or other hazardous tools should be performed by an adult.*

Feel free to devise your own methods of using the information in this book to increase the mutual creative enjoyment of working with a group of children.

ONE

Getting Started

....

A User's Guide to Organizational Tips and Inexpensive Materials

Later chapters in this book give step-by-step instructions for making a variety of puppets, masks, scenery, stages and sound effects. Detailed instructions are also given to guide you through three complete storytelling arts projects, from the initial construction of puppets, masks and scenery to the final performance of an international folktale.

Here are some practical suggestions to keep your storytelling arts project running smoothly:

- Puppet and mask construction involves a fair amount of messiness. Choose a work space which can support creative clutter. If children are going to use glue or paint, protect the space with newspaper, flattened grocery bags, plastic trash bags, old bedspreads, or discarded shower curtains. These will make cleanup much easier.

- Prepare an emergency bag. (Don't panic, this is for puppet emergencies—loose arms, wobbly control rods, etc.) A sturdy canvas bag or backpack works well. You may want to add other things to this bag as you become more experienced, but the following items will do for starters:

  duct tape
  clear plastic tape
  masking tape
  good pair of adult scissors
  sturdy stapler (pliers-type is best)
  bottle of white household glue
  (stored in a zipper-close plastic bag, to keep the emergency bag from becoming a sticky swamp)

- You may want to purchase an inexpensive cloth carpenter's apron. This clever garment ties around the waist and features several capable pockets for keeping stapler, scissors and tape right in front of you. When disaster strikes, you can whip out your stapler and reattach an ogre's ear before he knows what hit him.

- If you are working with a large group of children all making different kinds of puppets, masks and scenery at the same time, set up a separate work station for each type of creation. Make sure each work area has the materials needed to complete that type of storytelling aid.

- You can take a more gradual approach and arrange for small groups of children to work on their creations at different times, storing the completed puppets, masks and scenery until everything is complete and the entire group is ready to practice for the performance.

- If children will be making animal puppets or masks, display pictures of the animals. Visual references can be a great aid for children trying to reconstruct their own versions of the animals. If the storytelling aids are being constructed to dramatize a folktale from a particular country or culture, display illustrations from magazines or books showing the costumes, animals, landscapes, architecture and artwork of that country. (The public library is often a great source for these materials.) Such images may stimulate students to experiment with new patterns, shapes and color combinations.

- Use a portable hair drier if you need to shorten the drying time for projects using tempera paints, water-soluble crayons or papier-mâché.

- Children working on large puppets or sizable pieces of scenery will need a clear area of floor space.

- In addition to providing each work station with the materials necessary to complete specific projects, offer supplemental choices. A separate table accessible to all groups can be spread with optional materials. The following odds and ends offer many creative possibilities:

  feathers
  colorful cloth scraps
  crepe paper streamers
  tissue paper
  wrapping paper
  pipe cleaners
  glitter
  buttons
  construction paper
  ribbon
  yarn
  bells
  pompoms
  dried beans
  beads
  sequins
  cotton balls
  Christmas tree garlands
  tinsel
  artificial flowers
  geometric stickers (no bunnies or elves)

These materials can usually be obtained from craft and variety stores. Children can contribute decorating supplies from home as well.

- If several children will be needing tape for their projects and you are short on tape dispensers, attach small pieces of tape loosely to the edges of a table or around the edges of a bowl or storage tin. Children can then help themselves as needed.

- Children work at different speeds. Some will complete their creation with a few swift, bold moves, others will work for an hour or more, carefully adding one detail after another until they feel their puppet or mask is complete. For this reason, it is a good idea to have one or more group projects at each construction session. Point out these activities to the children before they start to work on their individual creations. When children finish their individual work, they can help with one of the group projects.

- In general, puppets and masks are most effective if features are exaggerated. A puppet's tiny button features may charm the close observer, but they fade to cryptic scratchings when viewed by a distant audience.

   There is an easy way to demonstrate this fact to the children before they begin work. Sketch simple facial features on two paper plates. Give one plate small controlled features; use big, bold and resolute lines to form the other plate's face. Stand some distance from the children, and hold up the two paper plates. Ask which face is easier to see.

- It is often helpful to show children a completed example of the type of puppet or mask they will be making, so they can see how it fits together. Demonstrate your completed creation before the children begin to work on their own. Talk about the decorating options open to them. Encourage children to develop their projects in whatever style pleases them. Then put your model away, so the young artists will not be tempted to copy your work.

- Doubled paper grocery bags make handy storage containers for completed masks and small puppets. They are also useful for organizing materials. Place the supplies for each group's project into a large doubled bag or bags. Write the name of the project on the outside bag. When the children are ready to begin their projects, simply whip out the appropriate bags of supplies and set out the contents. These double bags also make convenient storage containers for sorting project materials; cloth scraps can go into one, yarn into another. Roll the tops down to display the materials within. Cardboard boxes or canvas bags provide better storage for heavy supplies. Larger projects can be propped up in a corner or stored in a closet until needed. If you string a sturdy cord or wire overhead across a room, completed puppets and masks can be clipped to it with clothespins, combining convenient storage with attractive display.

Things to Think About

Allow yourself sufficient time to get organized. The better prepared you are, the more enjoyable the whole undertaking will be for you and the children. Although children enjoy being active participants in a creative activity, they do not enjoy waiting quietly and patiently while lengthy preparations are being made. If you are working with a small group of children, they may be able to help you gather materials and set up work stations. If you are working with a large group, advance preparation can make the difference between creative clutter and noisy chaos.

It is important to remember that the puppets, masks and scenery are meant to be a reflection of the *children's* imaginations. Assisting adults can encourage children and suggest that they consider a variety of design options and techniques, but they should not develop the children's creations for them. Adults enjoy having opportunities to cut, paste and paint, but a puppet is not really the child's creation if an overly helpful adult dictates its appearance. Too much help will also diminish the child's confidence and sense of accomplishment. Once children have been provided with the basic foundations, allow them the freedom to develop their creations in whatever style they find personally satisfying. If a child wants a fish puppet to have pink hair and a nose like a butternut squash—why not?

With this in mind, make it clear that children are not allowed to criticize each other's creations. Such criticism could rob a child of the joys of self-expression. Provide an atmosphere that is supportive of every child's work.

Unfortunately, some children may have already learned to mistrust their own artistic expression. They may come to you for advice or approval. Take this opportunity to point out that there is no right or wrong when it comes to artwork. Every person's work is unique; that's what makes it interesting.

Even with this support, some children may try to abandon their creativity. "I don't know how to draw a duck," they may say, "can you do it for me?" The following type of questioning can help to guide them out of such binds and provides a practical focus for their creative endeavors:

"Close your eyes. Now what do you see in your mind's eye when you think of a duck?"

"Here is a picture showing several ducks. What do they all have in common?"

"What shape is a duck's body? Beak? Feet?"

"What is it about a duck that makes it look different from a cow?"

"What color would you like your duck to be?"

"If you had a picture of a football, what would you have to add to make it look like a duck?"

"What can you do to make your duck look like your special duck?"

The duck doesn't have to look like a picture-postcard duck. It only has to convey the impression of a duck. Promote innovation. If the duck ends up wearing sunglasses and a fez, then that's a duck with real personal style!

What Materials to Use

In this section you will find general information about materials, how they can be used and where they can be obtained. Trial-and-error experimentation is an honorable method of discovery, but you can end up with your fingers glued together. The following advice is intended to save you time—and fingers.

Other materials will be discussed in the instructions for making specific puppets. It's fun to experiment with materials and discover new ways to use them. If you have doubts whether certain materials will work well together, try them out on a small scale before you begin working with children. As you gain experience, you will develop your own list of possibilities.

CARDBOARD

Heavyweight cardboard can be a valuable storytelling arts commodity, useful for scenery or large puppet parts. It is easy to obtain; simply slice down along the corner folds of any refrigerator or washing machine box. Presto! You are looking at four sheets of sturdy cardboard. It is inexpensive; store owners are usually only too happy to have you haul away their empty boxes. It is user-friendly; cardboard is lightweight, easy to work with and doesn't require specialized tools. It's versatile; it can be stiffened, folded, curved, stapled, cut, perforated, glued and painted.

If you are cutting a shape out of heavy cardboard, lay it on a piece of old carpeting or plywood to protect floors from the utility knife, or spread it out on a grassy lawn. Sturdy cardboard can also be cut with a serrated steak knife, if you don't mind a ragged edge on the cardboard and a somewhat dulled edge on the steak knife.

Cardboard can be stiffened and strengthened by applying a thin coat of white household glue to each side. (If you paint only one side, the cardboard will warp.) Better yet, add a mixture of white glue and white poster paint—one part glue to two parts paint. Whether or not you wish to fortify the cardboard with glue, you may want to add a base coat of white poster paint. Any colors the children add to cardboard with a white base coat will be brighter and more colorful than those painted directly onto the brown cardboard.

Large appliance, grocery and liquor stores are often good sources of cardboard boxes.

Poster board is thin cardboard that is stronger than paper yet more flexible than heavy cardboard. Use it to provide a strong, flexible foundation

for masks, puppets and scenery. Cutting and shaping is easily done with scissors. Poster board comes in black, white and assorted colors. It will accept all coloring agents.

Poster board is available in art supply, craft, stationery and variety stores.

Paper plates are a convenient and inexpensive source of thin cardboard, useful for many purposes. They can be stapled together to form mouth puppets, trimmed into stars or dragon claws, or transformed into quick-and-easy masks. They can be cut easily with scissors. Paper plates will accept all coloring agents. (Plastic plates do not.)

Two basic types of paper plates are called for in this book. The most common type is the inexpensive plain white paper plate, which is very flexible. The other type is a sturdier, rigid paper plate, which is somewhat more expensive.

Paper plates are available in grocery and paper product stores.

CUTTING TOOLS

Utility knives can effectively cut through heavy cardboard or foam rubber. Use with care, as the razor blades are very sharp. If they aren't, they should be; replace dull blades with new ones. *Cutting that requires a utility knife should be performed by an adult only. Store the knife in a safe place, and retract or remove the blade when not in use.*

This tool can be purchased at hardware and art supply stores.

Scissors are used to make many of the creations for storytelling projects. Get yourself a pair of sharp sturdy scissors. Young children should use safety scissors; the plastic type with metal cutting insets work pretty well. There will be some jobs that children's scissors just cannot handle, and that's when you can help out with your adult model.

Both types of scissors are available at hardware, stationery, art supply and variety stores.

Steak knives or other small, sturdy knives with a serrated cutting edge can be used effectively to cut through large pieces of cardboard. They leave ragged edges, unlike the clean cut made by a utility knife. Using a steak knife to cut cardboard will eventually dull the blade, so don't use a family heirloom. A steak knife is a good choice, to saw down along the corner edges of sturdy cardboard boxes, opening them up into sheets of flat cardboard. It can also be used in conjunction with a cutting board to saw Styrofoam into shapes. *This tool is recommended for adults and older children only.*

Steak knives are obtainable from any store selling eating utensils, the local thrift shop and probably your own kitchen drawer.

PAINTS AND COLORING AGENTS

Tempera paints are waterbase and provide bright colors on cardboard, paper, poster board, foam rubber or

cloth. They do not adhere well to plastic, Styrofoam or window shades. Basic colors can be blended and mixed to create a wide range of hues. These paints can be purchased in liquid form or in a dry powder that is mixed with water before use. When preparing paints, avoid adding too much water. Runny paint is hard to control and requires a longer drying time. Paints can be applied with paintbrushes, foam brushes or chunks of foam rubber.

Tempera covers large areas effectively. If it is used to decorate puppets, masks or scenery, allow for drying time before the items are used. Most objects decorated with tempera will dry sufficiently overnight. Allow longer drying time for painted foam rubber or anything painted with thin, runny paint. These paints clean up with water, but the task will be greatly shortened if the work area has been protected by newspapers or a plastic drop cloth.

Children can wear old long-sleeve shirts buttoned up the back as protective painting smocks. If these are unavailable, make your own smocks by cutting arm and head holes in the bottoms and sides of plastic garbage bags. (Children should roll up their sleeves when wearing this model.) *To avoid accidental suffocation, make sure the children do not put bags over their heads until the head and armholes have already been cut.* Any paint that ends up on children's clothing will usually come out in the wash.

Tempera paints are available at craft, art supply and most stationery stores.

Acrylic paints come in a wide variety of colors. They adhere to the same materials as tempera paints, but they are less likely to crack and peel after drying. Acrylics are, however, more expensive than tempera paints. They can be used to great advantage on special projects such as papiermâché masks. Paintbrushes can be cleaned easily with water.

Acrylic paints are available in art supply stores.

Crayons are inexpensive and easy to use. They can add color to paper, poster board and cardboard. If you use the sides of crayons after taking the paper sheaths off, you can cover fairly large areas with color. Their hues are not as vivid as paints, and they do not spread or blend as easily as oil pastels. They should not be used on anything delicate due to the pressure it takes to apply them.

Crayons are widely available. In fact, you probably have several crayons under your sofa cushions.

Water-soluble crayons are quite a bit more expensive than regular crayons, but they are more versatile. You can apply them dry, like crayons, then spread the colors with a wet paintbrush, or dip the end of a crayon into water and apply the color as flowing paint. The color adheres to paper, cardboard, Styrofoam, foam rubber, plastic, window shades and cloth. Working with small containers of water for dipping, these crayons are easy to use and less messy than paints.

They can be obtained at art supply stores.

Oil pastels are similar to crayons but produce stronger colors which can easily be spread and blended with the finger or a scrap of cloth. Oil pastels do, however, tend to smear and will rub off on hands and clothing, so use them only on objects which will not be handled extensively. The colors can be secured with fixatives, *but many fixatives can only be applied safely in well-ventilated areas. You may do well to avoid the potential health risks by not using fixatives when working with young children.* Oil pastels work well for drawing and coloring scenery. They adhere to paper, cardboard, window shades, Styrofoam and cloth. No drying time is required.

Oil pastels are available at art supply and most stationery stores.

Chalk can provide inexpensive, subtle color for paper, cardboard and cloth. It spreads easily but tends to rub off on hands and clothing; limit chalk art to things that will not be handled frequently. If a large chalkboard is available, children can use it to create a colored-chalk scenic background for their show. Use the type of chalk advertised as dustless and nontoxic when working with children.

Chalk is available in art supply and stationery stores.

Felt-tip markers provide vivid color, and they are easy to apply. They are not, however, practical for filling in large areas with color. Use them for detail work such as drawing the facial features of puppets. Water-base, not permanent, markers should be used when working with children. The water-base colors do not give off the noxious fumes of permanent markers. They bond to paper, poster board, cloth, cardboard and, to a limited extent, Styrofoam.

You can find felt-tip in stationery, art supply and variety stores.

STAPLERS

Pliers-type staplers, almost as invaluable as duct tape, are very useful tools for storytelling arts projects. This type of stapler is stronger and more versatile than a desktop stapler and can weasel its way into most hard-to-reach places. It offers a quick, strong, unobtrusive method of attaching various materials together. Make sure you know how to reload it before you begin your project, and keep extra staples on hand. This is the tool to use when a heavy-duty stapler is required.

Pliers-type staplers can usually be obtained at stationery and hardware stores.

Desktop staplers can also be useful if they are sturdily built, though they are more limited in reach and work best when placed on a firm, flat surface. Children may find this type of stapler easier to operate than the pliers type.

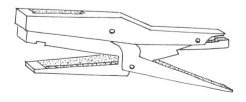

Pliers-type stapler

These are available at stationery, hardware and variety stores.

Long-reach staplers are a variation of the desktop stapler. A long-reach stapler can place a few strategic staples at the center of a paper-plate mask or along the entire length of a poster-board elephant leg. With its twelve-inch reach, it can provide a quick solution for otherwise difficult attachment dilemmas.

Long-reach staplers are usually sold at large stationery and office supply stores.

GLUE

White household glue is probably the only glue you will need for your project. This all-purpose glue bonds to paper, cloth, wood, foam rubber, Styrofoam and cardboard, yet cleans up easily while wet with a warm, damp cloth or sponge. The bond will be stronger and the drying time shorter if you use a small amount and spread it thinly. Be sure to share this fact with children, as they tend to follow the "more is better" philosophy of gluing. It is easy to recognize someone operating under this misconception—the work area is puddled with sticky white "tar pits."

Put the glue in small, broad-bottom containers and demonstrate how to apply dabs with cotton swabs. Glue can also be applied with small scraps of foam rubber or inexpensive paintbrushes. Clean the brushes well with soap and water after use.

Spring-type clothespins make handy clamps for many gluing jobs.

When gluing flat surfaces together, lay them on top of a drop cloth on the table or floor and weight them with books until the glue has dried. You can also brush a thin coat of white glue onto cardboard to make it stiffer and stronger.

You will find this type of glue at hardware, stationery and variety stores.

Glue sticks are neat and easy to use—no sticky puddles with these things. Unfortunately, the bond they create lacks strength. A glue stick can successfully bond together lightweight objects such as tissue paper, construction paper, crepe paper, glitter or short pieces of yarn, but don't rely on it to handle anything weightier.

Glue sticks are available at craft, stationery and variety stores.

TAPE

Duct tape is such a versatile, hardworking material that if the earth ever wobbled out of orbit, the problem could no doubt be remedied with a few strategically placed pieces. Strong, easy to use, flexible and relatively inexpensive, this stuff is great! It can repair breaks and tears, fortify stress points and wrap and strengthen weak or splintered puppet control rods. It cannot be covered up with paint or other coloring agents, however, so use it where it will not show.

It is sold at most hardware stores.

Clear plastic tape is handy for quick repairs where great strength is not required. This transparent tape can be used to attach decorations to puppets without the mess and drying time of glue. It can be used on a painted or colored surface without obscuring the design. Since paints and other coloring agents do not adhere well to it, make sure the area to be taped is already the desired color before tape is applied.

Clear tape is obtainable in most stationery, drug, grocery or variety stores.

Masking tape is a little stronger than clear plastic tape, and it will accept paint and felt-tip marker color to some extent. If you need to attach items to paper, cloth or cardboard with the intention of painting the final result, this is the tape to use.

Use masking tape to attach shapes to your underlying mask foundations, then cover it all with layers of papier-mâché.

Roll little pieces of this tape over on themselves (sticky side out) to create double-stick tape, which can be used to attach the backside of construction paper scenery to a cloth curtain.

Masking tape can be purchased from hardware or paint supply stores.

ASSORTED OTHER MATERIALS

Cloth offers many ideas for storytelling theater. Small pieces can be made into puppet bodies or used to decorate puppets and masks. Larger pieces can serve as bodies for big animal puppets or as costumes for mask wearers. Old sheets and lightweight bedspreads are good sources of material. A large white sheet can be decorated to serve as the main curtain.

Cloth can be decorated with tempera paints. Spread out large pieces to be painted on the floor on top of a plastic shower curtain or newspapers.

You can also add color and design to scenery cloth with oil pastels or felt-tip markers, or attach decorations (paper houses, tissue-paper grass, artificial flowers, etc.) with clear plastic tape or double-folded masking tape.

Cloth can be obtained from fabric stores, thrift stores and rummage sales. Parents of participating children are often willing to donate cloth for this type of arts project.

Window shades can be used as a foundation for scenic background. Children can draw directly onto the shades with oil pastels or water soluble crayons, or they can attach construction paper scenery with double-folded masking tape. The decorated shade can then be hung from a step ladder, a folding screen or a strong cord.

You may have a pile of neglected old window shades huddling in some forgotten corner of your attic or basement. New shades can be purchased at hardware stores.

Control rods come in many sizes, as do the puppets they operate. If a stiff, thin object is the desired length, strong enough to serve its purpose and smooth enough to avoid giving splin-

ters, it will make a good control rod. Small puppets can be operated with craft sticks or pencils. Craft sticks are available in two sizes. Large sticks (tongue-depressor size) provide a steadier rod; small sticks (Popsicle-stick size) are less expensive. Paint stirrers and rulers provide sturdier rods. Thin wooden dowels and bamboo plant stakes can serve as longer rods for lightweight puppets or scenery. The flat sticks at the bottom of old window shades make excellent control rods for larger puppets, as do yardsticks and wooden dowels. Broomsticks, mop handles and sturdy cardboard tubes make handy rods for the largest puppets. Lattice strips are another good source of flat wooden control rods when cut to the desired length.

Craft sticks can be purchased in craft stores. Pencils and rulers are available at stationery and variety stores. Paint stirrers, yardsticks and replacement handles for mops can be found at hardware stores. Bamboo plant stakes can usually be found at garden supply centers. Long, sturdy cardboard tubes can usually be had for the asking at upholstery or fabric stores. Lattice strips and wooden dowels can be purchased at lumberyards and some hardware stores.

Foam rubber is lightweight and durable. It will accept tempera paint as a coloring agent, if you allow plenty of drying time, and it can be cut and shaped with a utility knife or sharp scissors. Small chunks of foam rubber can be used as paintbrushes.

Foam rubber can usually be obtained at fabric or craft stores.

PVC plastic pipe is a lightweight, sturdy potential building material for some performance stages. Use a hacksaw or coping saw to cut the pipe to the desired length.

It can usually be obtained at hardware or plumbing supply stores.

Papier-mâché is inexpensive, messy and fun to use. It gives children the opportunity to develop sculpturing skills. Such objects as small boxes, Styrofoam and paper cups can be attached with masking tape to various puppet head foundations to add shape and dimension. Torn strips of paper dipped into paste can then be applied to cover and strengthen.

Wads of white bathroom tissue or paper towel can be dipped into the paste. After the excess paste is squeezed out, the wads can be applied to the structure and shaped much like clay. These will dry into a rough texture—perfect for warts and rough-featured characters. If you wish to use them to add body and shape but desire a smoother finish, cover them with a layer of dipped paper strips. When the papier-mâché dries (usually in two to five days), the puppet head can be painted. For more detailed instructions on using papier-mâché, see the *Saw-Toothed Lion* puppet in Chapter 3 and the *Papier-Mâché Mask* in Chapter 4.)

There are several ways to make papier-mâché paste. One popular method is to use cellulose wallpaper powder, but you can also make a flour paste of

1/2 cup flour to 1 cup water. The cellulose powder mixes easily with water (1 tablespoon powder to 1 cup water), it forms a smooth paste that dries clear, it will not stain clothing, and it washes off hands with water. *Cellulose paste is not, of course, meant to be taken internally, so do not use it when working with very young children, who might be tempted to taste it.* A little cellulose powder goes a long way—sucking up water like a longhaired dog on a hot summer day—so you may have to add more water if the paste gets too thick. The type of papier-mâché work recommended in this book involves no overnight soaking. Just mix up the paste and start dipping your torn paper strips.

Using a combination of two types of paper to dip in the paste works well. Overlapping strips of paper torn from brown paper grocery bags will give a papier-mâché project great strength. If strips of white (unprinted) newsprint are applied as the top layer of the project, they will dry into a smooth white surface, which will provide a light background for paints and other decorating materials. Always tear—do not cut—the paper you will be using for papier-mâché. Torn edges are easier to smooth down, making your seams less noticeable. Tearing paper with the grain will give you long strips, while tearing against the grain will give you odd-shape pieces.

A papier-mâché project takes from two to five days to dry. Drying time depends on the amount of papier-mâché paste used, the moisture level and temperature of the circulating air. You can hasten the drying time by putting the object outside in the sun on a hot, dry day or by using an electric blow drier.

Cellulose wallpaper paste can be purchased at hardware stores. Plain white newsprint can be found in art supply and educational supply stores.

PART TWO

PUPPETS AND MASKS

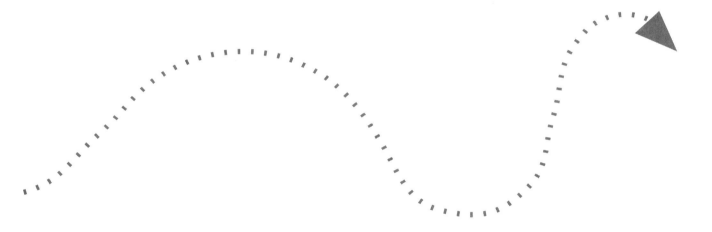

TWO

Small- to Medium-Size Puppets

Small but Spirited

When you encounter the word *puppet,* do you picture a sock-like affair with a squeaky little voice and lumpy head resembling a shriveled plum? Though this conventional puppet has its uses, it also has its limitations: it lacks versatility, has limited visual appeal, and can only be seen by a small audience sitting close to the puppet stage. Dramatic storytelling is more appealing when performed by a varied cast of puppets in assorted sizes, shapes and styles. When children are given a chance to explore these possibilities, their productions become a kaleidoscope of color and form that genuinely engages the imagination of their audience. Why settle for a polite audience sitting dutifully through a children's performance, when your audience could be completely involved and eager to see what happens next?

While large puppets are guaranteed to add visual spice and excitement to dramatic storytelling, small and medium-size puppets have distinct advantages of their own. They can be constructed easily at a table or desk, they do not require much performance space, and they can be stored in a grocery bag.

Before the children begin to work on their puppets, take some time to talk about what they're going to do. This will help spark their imaginations and focus them on the project. Show colorful pictures of the subjects involved—animals, insects or people in native costume. Mention the materials the children will be working with and talk about some of the different decorating options. While the children are working, you might want to play an appropriate recording as an evocative background sound, such as animal calls, bird songs or ethnic music.

Once the children have completed their puppets, give them time to experiment with puppet manipulation. Encourage them to move their own bodies in a way which mimes an activity or expresses an emotion, then ask them to imitate that same movement with their puppets. How would their puppets move if they were feeling sad? Happy? Excited? Frightened? Sleepy? Affectionate? Proud?

Children can construct these puppets to dramatize a story or to take part in a creative group activity. Why not roll up your sleeves and give the following puppets a try?

Vibrant Butterfly

This simple and colorful rod puppet gives children a chance to share in the pleasures of vicarious flight. Powered by an easy up-and-down movement of the hand, it flutters softly across the room, vibrating with color and pattern. A flock of these butterflies will add color and movement to any folktale dramatization—especially if the plot involves seasonal change.

PAVING THE WAY

Preparation Materials

9" x 12" piece of poster board

pencil

ruler

scissors

Construction Prep

1. Fold the poster board in half by bringing the 9" edges together.

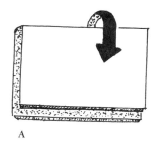

A

2. Open the paper up and mark two pencil dots along the fold line, each dot marking a point 3" in from one of the 12" edges. Using your ruler, draw a diagonal line from each dot to the nearest upper corner. Now draw a diagonal line from each dot to the nearest bottom corner.

3. Cut along the pencil lines and save the triangles for your scrap materials collection. You are left with a template for a butterfly. Round off the pointed corners for a softer shape.

If you are going to be working with a large group of children, you may want to make several templates.

Fold, measure and cut a section of poster board or thin cardboard to create this reusable butterfly template. Children can trace around the template to create colorful sets of aerodynamic construction paper wings.

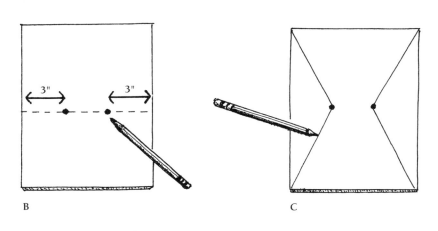

B

C

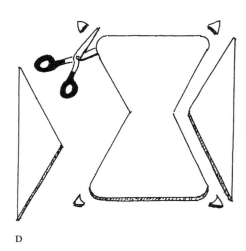

D

CHILDREN'S ACTIVITY

Materials

construction paper (one piece per puppet)

crayons or oil pastels in assorted colors

children's scissors

butterfly template(s)

large craft stick (tongue depressor) (one per puppet)

pipe cleaners (two per puppet)

pictures of butterflies (optional)

stapler

Preparing the Work Area

1. Place a sheet of construction paper at each child's place at a worktable. If you have a variety colors, leave them in a stack and let children choose their own.

2. Put crayons, scissors, butterfly template(s), craft sticks and pipe cleaners within easy reach at the center of the table.

3. Display butterfly pictures in a prominent place and keep the stapler nearby.

Completing the Project

1. Each child places the template on top of a piece of construction paper, traces around it, and cuts out the butterfly wings.

2. Give children time to decorate the wings in any style and colors they like. Encourage them to experiment with interesting patterns such as dots, stripes, geometric shapes and blocks of color. They can decorate both sides of the wings.

3. When the wings are finished, draw a small pair of eyes on the top front end of the craft stick.

4. Give each child two pipe cleaners, and have them cut both in half to make four pieces. (You may need to help out with a sharper pair of scissors.) Three of the pieces can be twisted around the center of the craft stick, with the ends left hanging down to represent six dangling insect legs. The fourth pipe cleaner half can be twisted around the front end of the stick with the ends left waving in the air over the butterfly's eyes, to form a pair of antennae.

5. Ask children to place their craft stick bodies under their butterfly wings, making sure that each craft stick projects a little from both the top and the bottom of the wings. The pipe cleaner legs should be hanging down and the antennae sticking up. Staple the wings to the craft sticks.

Animating the Puppet

If the child holds the tail end of the craft stick and moves the butterfly slowly up and down, air pressure will cause the butterfly's wings to flutter gracefully. Children can practice flying across the room with their butterflies.

Music is a welcome addition to such fanciful flights. Try playing a variety of music; the children can demonstrate how their puppets might dance and soar differently to fit the spirit of each tune, or let the children suggest what kind of music their butterflies would like to fly to. Try dividing the children into small groups to develop a simple choreography for their butterflies

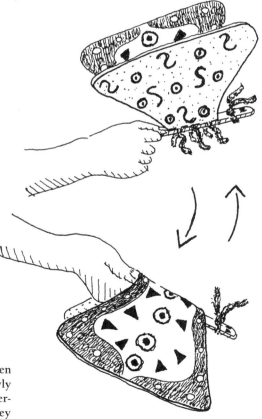

The butterfly's wings will lift and fall when the horizontal control rod is moved slowly up and down. Encourage children to experiment with puppet animation. Can they make their butterflies hover? Glide? Land softly on a paper flower?

Buzzing Bee

The control rod for this puppet doubles as a homemade kazoo, providing a vibrating hum for this industrious insect.

PAVING THE WAY

Preparation Materials

- **white household glue**
- **sturdy wooden toothpick**
- **two Styrofoam balls 1 1/2" in diameter (found in craft and hobby stores)**
- **wax paper**
- **scissors**
- **ruler**
- **cellophane (If unavailable, use wax paper)**
- **pipe cleaner**

Construction Prep

1. Dab a little white glue onto one end of the toothpick. Poke this end into the center of one of the Styrofoam balls. Keep pushing until half the toothpick's length is inside the ball. Dab glue onto the remaining half of the toothpick, then slide the other Styrofoam ball onto the projecting end. Keep pushing until the balls touch, forming a basic bee body. You will need one of these prepared bodies for each bee puppet.

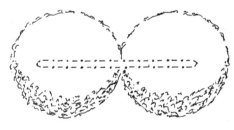

A toothpick binds two Styrofoam balls together forming the bee body.

2. Cut the wax paper into 4" x 4" squares, to create the vibrating surface for the kazoos. You will need one square for each bee kazoo. Cut the cellophane into 4" x 4" squares to be used for bee wings. You will need one cellophane square for each bee. (If you have no cellophane, use wax paper for this square also.)

3. Cut a pipe cleaner into several 1 1/2" sections, to be used later as bee antennae. You will need a pair of these short sections for each puppet.

CHILDREN'S ACTIVITY

Materials

- pictures of bees (optional)
- prepared bee body (one per puppet)
- tissue paper in assorted colors
- children's scissors
- short sections of pipe cleaner (two per puppet)
- white household glue
- cardboard tube from bathroom tissue, or half of a paper-towel tube (one per puppet)
- felt-tip markers in assorted colors
- cellophane or wax paper wing squares (one per puppet)
- 12" pipe cleaner (one per puppet)
- wax paper squares (one per puppet)
- rubber band (one per puppet)
- sharp nail

Preparing the Work Area

1. Set up the worktable, placing a bee body at each child's space. Put the tissue paper, children's scissors, short sections of pipe cleaner and glue supplies within easy reach of all. Display the bee pictures, if available, where everyone can see them.

2. Set aside cardboard tubes, felt-tip markers, wax paper and cellophane squares, full-length pipe cleaners, nail and rubber bands nearby.

Completing the Project

1. Have the children attach tissue-paper eyes, stripes, dangling legs, etc. to their Styrofoam bees with small dabs of white glue. They can either cut these shapes out of the tissue paper with scissors or tear the paper into the desired shapes. Poke two short sections of pipe cleaner into the top of the bee's head to serve as antennae. A small dab of glue will secure them.

2. When students have finished decorating their bee bodies, give each child a cardboard tube, and set out the felt-tip markers. The children can add colorful designs to the tubes.

3. As children finish, help them assemble their bee-kazoos. Fold the cellophane square in half, and pinch the two longer edges of the cellophane rectangle together in the middle, to form a set of wings. Wrap one end of a 12" pipe cleaner around this wing pinch to hold it. Now place the wings against the bee's back, and wrap the free end of the pipe cleaner around the bee's waist 1 1/2 times, so that pipe cleaner hangs down below the bee's body. Loop the dangling end of the pipe cleaner around the middle of the cardboard tube and secure it with a twist. Adjust the wings if necessary.

4. To add the kazoo effect, place the center of the wax-paper square flat against the forward end of the tube (the end under the bee's head). Press the surplus paper against the sides of the tube and secure with the rubber band; the wax paper should be tight and smooth across the tube opening. Use the nail to poke a hole in the top of the cardboard tube near the wax-paper end of the tube but not covered by the wax paper. *Safety Note: Do not allow young children to make their own nail holes. An adult should perform this step.*

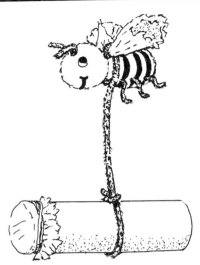

A single pipe cleaner will secure the wings to the bee and the bee to the cardboard tube. Narrow strips of tissue paper or six short sections of pipe cleaner can serve as the legs.

Animating the Puppet

Have the puppeteers hold their bee tubes over their heads. As they move across the room, the bees dart and vibrate on their pipe cleaners, appearing to have a life of their own. When sound effects are desired, the puppeteers can place the open end of the tubes over their mouths. They should then open their mouths into an O shape, pressing the outsides of their lips against the inside edges of the tube while saying "Aaaaaaaaah." Blowing will not produce the desired effect—and may send the wax paper sailing across the room. The idea is to get the wax paper vibrating, thereby producing a convincing buzzing sound. Give students time to practice their kazoo technique. If a child appears to be getting frustrated, remove the wax paper and encourage that child to make loud buzzing sounds. The tube will act as a megaphone.

Variations

• If you provide the children with 4" x 4" cardboard templates, they can trace around these squares on both the wax paper and the cellophane. Using children's scissors, they can cut out these materials for themselves.

Contemplative Fish

This rod puppet has a movable lower jaw—the better to blow imaginary bubbles with. This fish plays the title role in the Finnish folktale *Why Fish Can't Sing* (See Chapter 9).

PAVING THE WAY

Preparation Materials

- four 14" x 11" pieces of white poster board
- ruler
- sharpened pencil
- scissors
- white household glue
- glue brush
- large book or other heavy object
- large craft stick
- duct tape
- medium-size nail or Phillips screwdriver with a narrow shaft
- paper fastener
- pipe cleaner
- unsharpened pencil or chopstick

Construction Prep

1. Draw a pointy-nose fish on a 14" x 11" section of poster board. You can concoct one of these fellows by drawing a lemon with bulbous ends. The lemon should be about 12" long and 5" wide. Add a triangular tail, a couple of curved fins and a semicircular eye bulge to the outline of the lemon shape. On an unused portion of the poster board, draw a 3" x 1" cigar-shape object for the fish's movable lower jaw. Use the scissors to cut out the fish and lower jaw pieces.

2. The fish as is would be too flexible. Spread a thin layer of glue over the entire upper surface of the fish and that of its lower jaw. Then flip them over,

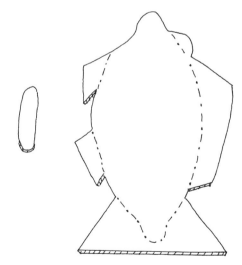

This is the basic shape for the fish and its movable lower jaw piece. You can play with the design, though you may want to use the suggested measurements at first.

glueside down, onto another section of poster board. Place a large book or other weighty object on top of the separate fish and jaw pieces to improve the bonding. Allow to dry.

3. Remove the book and cut around the fish and lower jaw.

4. Spread a little glue along the length of one flat side of the craft stick, leaving the last 2" free of glue. Press the glued portion of the stick against the center section of the fish tail, with the unglued part of the stick protruding from the tail. Add a strip of duct tape to reinforce the glue.

5. Place the lower jaw piece on top of the fish so that 1/3 of its length (about 1") protrudes from the fish opposite the bulging eye. Use your nail or screwdriver to poke a hole through both the fish and its overlapping jaw about 1/2" from the edge of the fish and halfway along the length of the jaw piece. Push a paper fastener through this hole from the underside, and press

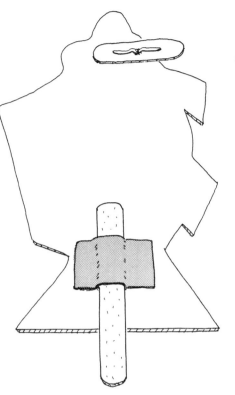

Most of the control rod overlaps the fish body to provide additional stiffness. Only one inch of the cigar-shape fish jaw will be seen by the audience; the rest extends behind the fish body to provide a pivotal purchase for the control rod.

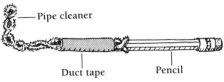

Pipe cleaner
Duct tape   Pencil

Prepared control rod

its flanges open so that they are parallel to the jaw piece.

6. Bend the pipe cleaner in half and twist together. Tape half of the length of this doubled pipe cleaner to one end of the unsharpened pencil or chopstick. Bend the top 1 1/2" of the protruding pipe cleaner into a right angle with the pencil.

CHILDREN'S ACTIVITY

Materials

- **Prepared fish body (one per puppet)**
- **felt-tip markers or crayons in assorted colors (metallic crayons are a nice option)**
- **white household glue**
- **brightly colored paper or sequins**
- **pencil-pipe cleaner control rods (one per puppet)**
- **duct tape**

Preparing the Work Area

1. Place a prepared fish stickside down at each child's workplace (they will not be decorating the side with the stick and the duct tape). Put markers or crayons at the center of the table or where they will be accessible to all.

2. Have glue, paper, sequins, duct tape and pencil control rods nearby.

Completing the Project

1. The children can decorate their fish with markers or crayons in whatever style they please. Suggest that they experiment with different colors and patterns. If the children are making these fish to dramatize *Why Fish Can't Sing* (See Chapter 9), encourage them to emphasize the eye of their puppets.

2. When students have finished, add the paper, sequins and glue to the table supplies. The children can use these materials to make decorative fish scales. Remind them that a small amount of glue works best.

Once the glue is dry, add the control rod for the lower jaw. Flip the fish over so its decorated side faces down. Position the pencil-pipe cleaner control rod on top of the fish so that the top 1 1/2"of doubled pipe cleaner overlaps the 1 1/2" of the lower jaw piece, and tape it firmly in this position with small pieces of duct tape. *Make sure you do not tape the lower jaw to the fish body, as this will interfere with free movement of the jaw.*

If you move the pencil up and down in line with the fish's body, the puppet's mouth should open and close. If the jaw movement is too stiff, rotate the lower jaw around its paper fastener with your hand until you have enlarged the hole a little and the jaw moves freely.

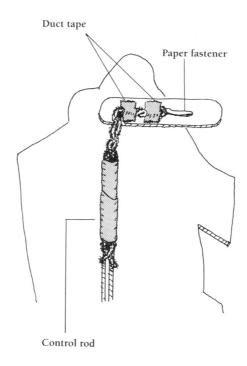

Make sure the jaw piece swivels freely around the paper fastener. Then attach the control rod.

Animating the Puppet

The fish is held in front of the body, with the decorated side facing out. The craft stick is held in one hand while the jaw control rod is operated with the other. Children can make this puppet dive and dart, undulate slowly as it swims, and stand on its tail while opening and closing its mouth. If the fish are used to dramatize a story, remind the children to keep the decorated sides of their puppets facing their audience, and give the children an opportunity to practice coordinating their hand movements. Ask the children what they think it would feel like to be a fish. How is moving through the water different from moving through the air?

Variation

• When you are making the fish shape out of poster board, try leaving off the tail and fin shapes. The children can make their own fish tails and fins from tissue paper or colorful cloth. These flexible tails and fins will wave and flow with a watery movement when the puppets are moved about.

Boisterous Chicken

She flaps, she flutters, she perches and she pecks. This rod puppet does everything but lay an egg.

Preparation Materials

- 28" x 22" sheet of white poster board
- pencil
- ruler or measuring tape
- scissors
- 8 1/2" x 11" sheet of typing paper
- dinner-size, sturdy, rigid paper plate
- flat wooden control rod at least 12" long (a thin wooden ruler works great)
- stapler or white household glue

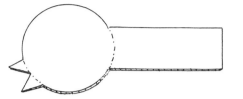

Suggested shape for the chicken head.

Construction Prep

1. Draw a simple chicken head on the poster board: Make a 4" circle, add a triangular beak, and finish with a 2" x 5" neck rectangle. Cut out the head.

2. Fold the typing paper in half, to a 5 1/2" x 8 1/2" size. Draw a line connecting a fold corner to a corner diagonally across from it. Cut along this line, cutting through both layers at once. The two smaller triangles will form the chicken's wings. The large triangle may be cut along the fold line to form an extra set of wings.

3. Fold the paper plate in half, with the eating surface of the plate on the inside. This folded plate will become the chicken's body.

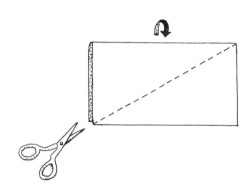

Plain white typing or computer printer paper provides inexpensive, lightweight wing material for small bird puppets. Fold and cut as shown for flexible, unadorned wings.

4. Place the chicken's head next to the wooden control rod so that 2" of the neck overlap one end of the control rod. Staple the neck to the rod in this position.

5. Position the head-rod unit inside the folded plate so that 3" of rod (the end without the chicken head) project from the back end of the chicken. The rod should be up near the plate's fold line. Secure the head-rod unit firmly in this position with several staples or glue. Leave the bottom edges of the folded plate open.

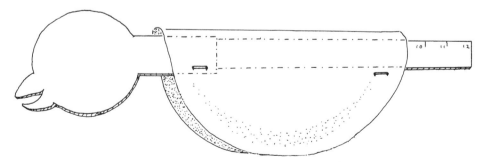

Use glue or staples to secure the rod to the plate. Leave the bottom edges of the plate open to give the chicken a broad base and a plump, well-fed look.

Materials

- prepared chicken (one per puppet)
- prepared wings (one pair per puppet)
- felt-tip markers in assorted colors
- pictures of chickens showing combs and feet (optional)
- red and yellow construction paper
- children's scissors
- clear plastic tape
- white household glue
- feathers (Children can make feathers out of construction paper if real feathers are not available.)
- stapler (pliers-type works best)

Preparing the Work Area

1. Set up a worktable with a chicken and a set of wings at each child's place. Put markers in the middle of the table. Prominently display chicken pictures, if available.

2. Place construction paper, children's scissors, clear plastic tape, glue and feathers at a convenient location nearby.

Completing the Project

1. Decorate the chicken bodies and wings with the markers. Encourage the children to experiment, drawing lines or other designs which give the impression of a feathered surface. Once the children have finished decorating the wings, set them aside to be attached later.

2. Put the construction paper, scissors, clear plastic tape and glue on the work table. Tell the children they can use these materials to make a comb (a rooster's comb is bigger than a hen's) and set of feet for their chickens. These can be attached to the puppets with clear plastic tape or glue. If desired, the children can also make construction paper wattles (you know, those baggy red wobbly lobes which dangle from chickens' chins and are—no doubt—very appealing to other chickens).

3. As a final flourish, bring out the feathers for tail ornamentation. If you were unable to obtain feathers, children can make them out of construction paper: Cut slender oval shapes out of paper, then cut several little slits or notches along both sides to "feather" them. Caution the children against attaching any feathers to the chicken's middle back area, because the wings will soon be positioned there.

4. After the chickens have received their tail plumage, attach the paper wings to the birds as follows. Place the bottom 5 1/2" edge of each wing against the middle upper side of the chicken—one on either side—with the wing points reaching up over the chicken's back. Staple the bottom of each wing firmly in place. Press the wings open gently, *without creasing them.*

Use glue or staples to attach the bottom edge of each wing to the paper plate body.

Animating the Puppet

Grab the control rod at the back end of the chicken. With the puppeteer providing the appropriate clucking sounds, the chicken can scratch and scurry around a tabletop as it searches for food. Rock it forward to peck at the ground. Rock it back and give a hearty crow. Lift the puppet from the table with a squawk, and move the rod up and down to display a startled hen fluttering her wings in alarm.

Bird-in-the-Hand

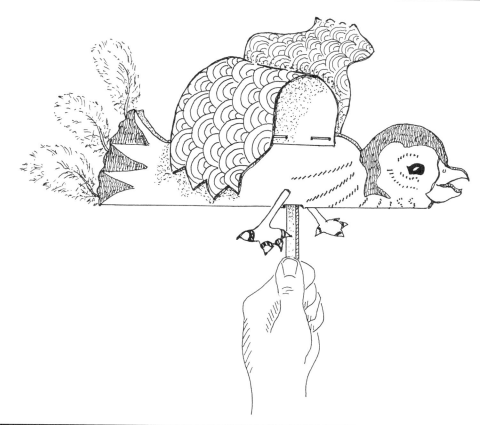

A smaller version of the High-Flying Bird described in Chapter 3, this inexpensive rod puppet plays a role in the Finnish folktale *Why Fish Can't Sing* (See Chapter 9).

PAVING THE WAY

Preparation Materials

- plain, flexible white paper plate
- pencil
- scissors
- white household glue
- glue brush
- craft stick (small or large)
- a heavy book or several spring-type clothespins
- 8 1/2" x 11" sheet of white bond paper
- ruler

Construction Prep

1. Fold the paper plate in half with the eating surface of the plate on the inside. Draw a simple bird body with the fold line forming the bird's belly.

2. Cut away any excess paper plate, cutting through both halves of the plate at once. Cut a 1" slit along the fold line near the middle of the bird's body.

3. Spread open the double bird and brush a thin coat of glue on its inside surfaces. Refold the bird, and push

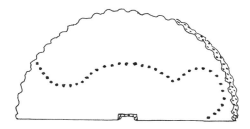

Incorporate the fold line into the bird's shape and cut a 1" slit in its center.

1" or 2" of the craft stick into the slit. Press the matching bird body parts together. Weight the bird with a heavy book or clamp it together with several spring-type clothespins until the glue dries.

4. Fold the sheet of white paper in half and draw a 7" x 3" rectangle. Cut out this shape, cutting through both layers of paper, to obtain matching rectangular wings. Round off one of the 3" ends of each wing, forming the wing tips.

CHILDREN'S ACTIVITY

Materials

- **prepared bird body (one per puppet)**
- **prepared wings (one pair per puppet)**
- **felt-tip markers in assorted colors**
- **children's scissors**
- **construction paper in various colors**
- **small feathers (if available)**
- **clear plastic tape**
- **white household glue**
- **stapler**

Preparing the Work Area

1. Set up a worktable, placing a bird and a set of wings at each child's space. Spread out markers and scissors along the center of the table.

2. Place construction paper, feathers, clear plastic tape, glue and a stapler in a convenient location.

Completing the Project

1. Children can decorate their birds and bird wings with the felt-tip markers, using whatever color combinations or feather patterns they wish. For added effect, use scissors to remove small triangles of paper from the rounded tips of the wings; the remaining zigzags will resemble the tips of the primary feathers.

2. Once decorated, set the wings aside. Add the construction paper, scissors, tape and glue to the table. Invite the children to design a set of feet and a beak for their birds. Students should cut out the feet and beak and glue them to their creations.

3. Place the feathers, if available, on the table. The children can glue or tape them to their birds' tails or add a few plumes to the top of the birds' heads: Dip the ends of the feather shafts in glue and insert into the slit between the plate halves, or simply tape the feathers to the outsides of the birds' body. *Feathers should not be added to the wings, because the additional weight would make them too heavy to flap.* The birds' backs

should also remain free of feathers, to facilitate the attachment of the wings. If feathers are unavailable, the children can make their own by cutting oblong feather shapes out of construction paper and cutting slits or serrations into the sides.

4. Assist the children in attaching a set of wings to their birds. These should be placed one on each side of the bird, with the straight 3" bottom edge halfway up the bird's side, and the rest of the wing reaching up over the bird's back. Staple each bottom edge securely in this position. Press the wings open gently without creasing them.

Animating the Puppet

If the children hold onto the craft sticks and move their hands slowly up and down, their birds' wings will flap gracefully. Give the birds some practice in taking off, climbing, flying around the room, gliding and landing on the edge of a table or desk.

Animal Mouth Puppet

With a couple of paper plates and a scrap of material, children can create any animal they choose—from snake to stegosaurus.

PAVING THE WAY

Preparation Materials

- **two plain, flexible white paper plates**
- **scissors**
- **stapler**
- **piece of lightweight cloth**
- **ruler**

Construction Prep

1. Fold one of the paper plates in half; open it up, and cut along the fold line.

2. Lay the uncut plate bottom-up in front of you on the table. Cover this plate with the two half pieces of plate, also bottom-up, matching the edges. Staple the two plates together every 2" or 3" all around the outside edges of the two plates.

3. Fold the double plate in half, with the fold following along the cut lines of the plate halves and the two half-plate sections on the outside (the uncut plate will be on the inside). Slide your hand into the plate pockets, with four fingers in the top pocket and your thumb in the bottom pocket. With the plate contraption on your hand, bring your fingers toward your thumb, then away. The paper plate mouth puppet will respond by smacking its lips together in a satisfying manner.

4. Cut the cloth into a square about 12" x 12". You will need one cloth body for each puppet. If possible, prepare a large assortment of cloth squares in different colors and patterns, and give each child a choice.

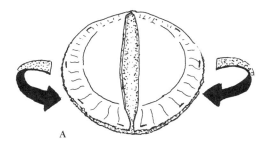
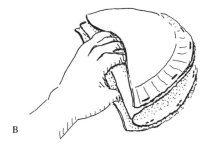

A   B

Place the paper plate halves on top of the uncut plate, staple together around the edges and fold.

35

Materials

- **prepared double plate (one per puppet)**
- **square of cloth (at least one per puppet)**
- **felt-tip markers in assorted colors**
- **construction or tissue paper in various colors**
- **children's scissors**
- **clear plastic tape**
- **white household glue**
- **stapler**

Preparing the Work Area

1. Set up a table with a prepared plate at each child's work space. Place colorful paper, scissors, tape, glue and felt-tip markers in the center of the table, where they can be easily reached.

2. Store the squares of cloth and the stapler nearby.

Completing the Project

1. Explain to the children that they will each have an opportunity to make an Animal Mouth Puppet. They can be deciding what kind of animal to make while you demonstrate how to operate this type of puppet. If you developed a sample animal puppet, use this for your demonstration. If not, place your hand inside one of the prepared double plates and show students how to operate the puppet's mouth. Drape a square of cloth over your arm to

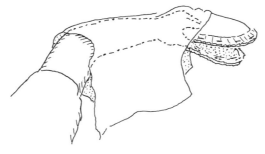

Attach a square of cloth to the top plate half with staples or tape. If there are any staple prickles on the inside of the finger slot, cover them with tape for the safety and comfort of the puppeteer.

demonstrate how the operating arm becomes the puppet's body.

2. Let each child choose a piece of cloth from the cut squares and place it near the prepared double plate. Explain that the top plate half can be developed into the animal's upper face (eyes, nose, top lip, etc.), with the eyes drawn just below the area where the cloth is to be attached. Then students can lift up the top plate half and decorate the inside of the animal's mouth.

The children can develop their critters to suit their imaginations. They can use the felt-tip markers to draw facial features directly onto the plates or cut features such as tongues, ears, whiskers, teeth and eyes out of the colored paper and attach them to the puppet with glue or tape. A puppet made using a combination of techniques can be especially appealing.

3. While the children are working on their puppets, help each child staple one edge of the cloth to the straight cut

edge of the top half plate. Be careful not to staple the finger slot closed. Excess cloth can hang over a little at both sides.

Animating the Puppet

Help the children place their puppets on their hands—fingers in the top slot, thumbs in the bottom slot, with the cloth draped over their arm. Show them how to make their puppets' mouths open and close. Ask students what sounds their animals might make. If these puppets are to be used in a dramatization, advise the puppeteers to tilt the backs of their hands forward, so the face of each puppet will be seen more clearly by the audience.

Encourage children to experiment with voice and movement. Can the puppet pick up a large paper wad with its mouth? Can it tell you what its favorite things are? How does it act when it is afraid of something? Happy? Asleep? Can it sing? Can it crawl up one side of a desk and slide down the other?

Variation

- The children may make construction paper legs for their animals (unless they choose to make snakes or earthworms). Glue or staple these paper legs to the sides of the cloth animal body. These little legs, dangling from either side of the puppeteer's arm, are downright irresistible!

Person Mouth Puppet

Add another paper plate and a construction paper body to transform your animal mouth puppet into a colorful citizen from any time or place. Constructing this puppet can encourage children to explore different cultures, costumes and languages. Create a world of people to help tell the story *Why Fish Can't Sing* (See Chapter 9).

PAVING THE WAY

Preparation Materials

- three plain, flexible white paper plates
- scissors
- stapler
- pencil
- 18" x 12" sheet of construction paper

Construction Prep

1. Using two of the paper plates, complete "Construction Prep" steps one through three of the *Animal Mouth Puppet* (page 35).

2. Put the paper plate puppet head on your hand as described. Place the third paper plate over the top plate half, matching the edges. It should cover the half plate (which houses your four fingers) and extend out over the back of your hand. Staple this third plate to the top half plate along the curved edges. (Make sure you are not stapling the puppet's mouth closed, and watch out for those fingers.)

(Right) Attach the third paper plate to the "upper lip" of the mouth puppet.

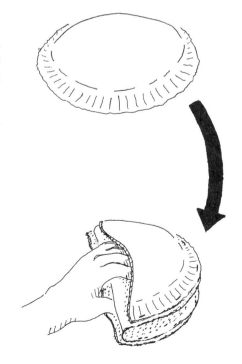

3. The section of plate which extends over the back of your hand will become the upper face of the Person Mouth Puppet. Fold this section forward until it stands up off your hand. Mark a tiny ✕ on the center of the front top edge of this plate, to indicate the top of the puppet's head.

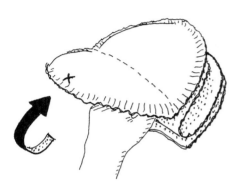

Push the back half of the top plate forward until it stands up off your hand. Marking a small x on top of the puppet's head will help orient children when they begin to develop their puppets.

4. On a full sheet of construction paper, draw a simple, headless human form—basically a plumped-up stick figure with two legs, two arms, simple mitten-shape hands and a long neck. Give the body an elongated neck, about 2" or 3" long. The entire body should be as tall as the length of paper allows. Cut out the headless form, which will serve as the puppet's body. Prepare several of these bodies in assorted colors so children can have a choice.

5. This puppet may seem confusing at first to some children. You might want to complete a demonstration puppet so students can see how it all fits together.

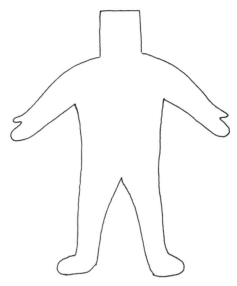

A simplified construction paper body can be decorated and developed by children to reflect any national costume or historical period.

CHILDREN'S ACTIVITY

Materials

- prepared three-plate head foundation (one per puppet)
- felt-tip markers in assorted colors
- tissue paper in assorted colors
- children's scissors
- clear plastic tape
- glue sticks
- lightweight decorating materials such as feathers, crepe paper streamers, geometric stickers, paper flowers, tinsel
- prepared puppet body (one per puppet)
- stapler
- pictures of people in different traditional costumes (optional)

Preparing the Work Area

1. Set up a table with a prepared puppet head at each child's work space. Place markers, clear plastic tape, glue sticks, tissue paper and scissors in the center of the table, within reach of all.

2. Place decorating materials, stapler and prepared puppet bodies nearby in a convenient location.

3. If you would like the puppets to represent a specific culture, display pictures of people in traditional costume.

Completing the Project

1. Pick up one of the prepared heads and demonstrate how it can be operated as a mouth puppet. Show children where the puppeteer's fingers and thumb fit in. Point out the inside of the mouth, the face area and the × which marks the top of the puppet's head. (If you have completed a demonstration puppet, this would be a good time to show it to the children). Let students know that they will be given a puppet body after they have decorated a puppet head.

Encourage children to draw their puppets' eyes first, as this will help to orient them. The eyes should be placed on the top half of the top plate just below the ×. The nose can be drawn below the eyes, in the central area of the top plate. The top lip is best located on the curved bottom edge of this plate. When the face is finished, children can lift the top plate and decorate the inside of the puppet's mouth.

Hair, tongues, mustaches and hats can be cut out of tissue paper and attached to the puppet heads with tape or glue. Add lightweight decorations to the table to offer additional choice in puppet design.

2. When children finish with the heads, they can choose a construction paper body. Tissue paper, felt-tip markers and lightweight decorations can be used to develop clothing and costumes for these bodies.

As students complete their puppets, show them how to staple the paper bodies to the puppet heads. The top section of each paper neck should be stapled to the bottom half plate of the head at a central location next to the open edge of the thumb slot. Cover the staples with tape. The puppet body should hang down from the head. Make sure the staples and tape do not interfere with the operation of the puppet's mouth or the use of its thumb slot.

Animating the Puppet

Remind the children to place four fingers in the top slot and a thumb into the bottom slot to operate the puppet mouth. Make sure each puppet's forehead and upper face area is pressed forward, forming a right angle with the lower face and mouth. Children can experiment with different voices until they find one which sounds just right. Encourage students to watch their puppets while they are learning to use them. Children can practice opening and closing their puppets' mouths while they are speaking, and holding still when listening to other puppets.

If these puppets are to be used to supplement a study of different cultures, they can take turns teaching each other about the customs and language of their homelands.

Variations

• Make the puppet's body from thin felt or stiff, lightweight cloth for greater durability.

• Make several basic body shapes out of poster board. Let children use these as templates or guides, and give students time to make their own paper or felt puppet bodies.

• If you are planning to use these puppets to dramatize *Why Fish Can't Sing* (Chapter 9), display pictures of people and costumes from around the world. After children have completed their puppets, have them practice teaching their puppets to say "Hello" in different languages.

Hand-Mouth Puppet

Another version of the paper plate mouth puppet, this whimsical creature supplements its generous oral equipment with the expressive gestures of the human hand. Use this puppet to dramatize *The Ogre's Staircase* or *The Singing Drum* (See Chapter 9).

PAVING THE WAY

Preparation Materials

- **three plain, flexible white paper plates**
- **sharp scissors**
- **stapler**
- **pencil**
- **piece of colorful lightweight cloth large enough to cut two 16" x 22" pieces**
- **duct tape, needle and thread, or sewing machine**

Construction Prep

1. Build a mouth puppet head using three paper plates, as described in "Construction Prep" steps one through three of *Person Mouth Puppet* (page 37).

2. Cut two matching cloth tunic pieces according to the measurements shown in the illustration.

3. Place one tunic piece on top of the other, matching the edges, with the best-looking side of each piece on the inside. Attach the two pieces together along their edges, leaving open the neck, bottom and arm holes. You can do this with staples, duct tape, needle and thread or sewing machine. If you use staples, feel the stapled seams with your hand to check for any sharp or scratchy staples. Cover these with small pieces of tape to protect the puppeteer from scratches.

4. Cut a 12" slit in the back of the tunic—(*do not cut through both layers of cloth*)—starting from the center bottom of the back piece of the tunic. This will allow the tunic to hang naturally when the child's arm is inserted for puppet head manipulation. Place a strip of duct tape at the top of the slit to prevent the material from ripping further along the cut line. Turn the tunic right-side out and admire the fetching little garment you have just produced.

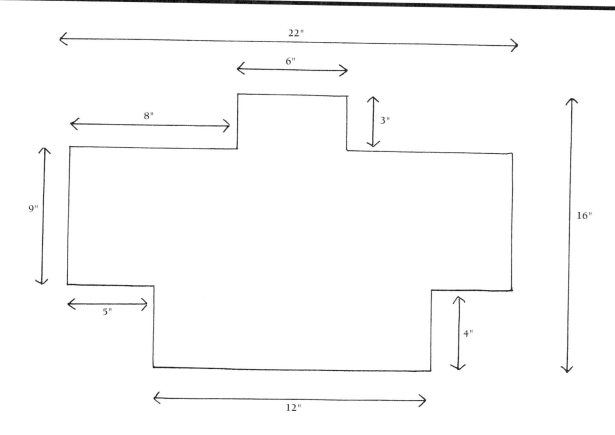

22"

6"

8"

3"

9"

16"

5"

4"

12"

Cut both the front and back tunic sections to this shape.

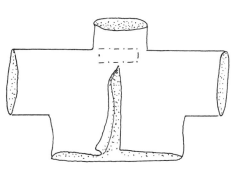

Cut a slit in the center of the back section of tunic and place a piece of reinforcing duct tape across the top of the slit on the inside of the tunic, where it will not show. (Do not cut the front section of the tunic.)

5. Slide your hand through the back slit of the tunic, and push it out through the top of the neck hole. Place the prepared paper plate puppet head on your hand, sliding your four fingers well into the top slot and your thumb into the bottom slot. (The uncut paper plate with the × should be uppermost on your hand.) With your free hand, hold a section of cloth from the front top edge of the tunic's neck against the cut edge of the bottom paper plate half (the area of plate right under your thumb). Wiggle your hand free from the puppet head and the tunic while continuing to hold the front edge of the neck hole in position. Staple the tunic neck to the head where you are holding them together, making sure you do not staple the thumb slot closed. Cover any scratchy staple points on the inside of the tunic with tape.

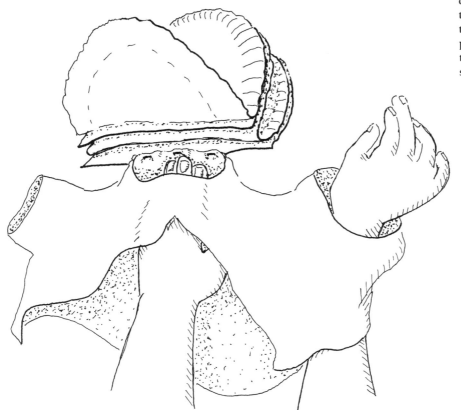

Staple the paper plate hand to the end of one of the sleeves, and staple the front of the tunic neck opening to the cut edge of the bottom plate-half. Slide one hand into the puppet's unused sleeve and the other through the neck tube and into the finger and thumb slots.

CHILDREN'S ACTIVITY

Materials

- plain, flexible white paper plate (one per puppet)
- felt-tip markers in various colors
- children's scissors
- prepared puppet head with attached tunic (one per puppet)
- clear plastic tape
- white household glue
- construction and tissue paper in various colors
- lightweight decorating materials such as small feathers, geometric stickers, crepe paper streamers, curling ribbon, yarn, origami paper (optional)
- stapler

Preparing the Work Area

1. Set up a table with felt-tip markers and children's scissors within reach of all. Place a white paper plate at each child's work space.

2. Set aside clear plastic tape, glue, puppet heads with attached bodies, paper, optional decorations and stapler for later use.

Completing the Project

1. Have each child place a hand flat on a paper plate and trace around it. Cut out the hand shape and set it aside for later use.

2. Place a prepared puppet head with attached tunic on your hand; if you have completed a demonstration puppet, use it instead. Demonstrate the puppet to the children, pointing out the movable mouth and the face area. Show them the × which marks the top of the puppet's head.

Encourage the children to draw the eyes of their puppets first, as this will help keep them oriented. Eyes should be placed on the top half of the top plate, slightly below the ×. Draw the nose in the central area of the top plate. The top lip is best located on the curved bottom edge of this plate. When the face is finished, children can lift the top plate and decorate the inside of the puppet's mouth.

3. As students complete their work with markers, place the colored paper, tape, glue and lightweight decorations (if available) on the table. Tell the children that they can use these supplies to construct hats, earrings, hair and other embellishments for their puppets.

4. As children finish decorating their puppets, assist them in putting the puppets on their hands—showing them how to push one hand through the slit in the back of the tunic, up through and out of the neck hole, and

into the finger and thumb slots. Make sure they understand where their fingers and thumbs should go and how to open and close the puppet's mouth when it is speaking. Once students feel confident about this, suggest they try putting their free hand up through the bottom opening in the tunic and out through the appropriate sleeve opening. That hand now becomes the puppet's hand, and puppeteers can add gestures to their speech. Slide the wrist end of the paper plate hand (which the puppeteer made earlier) into the puppet's empty sleeve, and staple the hand to the sleeve. This hand is just for looks and cannot be operated—unless the puppeteer is an octopus.

Animating the Puppet

Give children time to find a satisfying voice for their puppet, and to practice opening and closing the puppet's mouth when speaking. Encourage them to enliven the puppet's speech with expressive gestures. Remind them to focus on the puppet, to direct all their movements through the puppet, to communicate different emotions with head and hand positions— observing which movements are most effective. If possible, let children practice in front of a mirror.

Suggest activities which will give puppeteers a chance to activate their puppets. The puppets might introduce themselves, exchange greetings and shake hands with neighboring puppets, describe an exciting event or adventure, or play an imitative game like *Simon Says*.

If the puppets will be used to dramatize a story, remind children to tip the puppet heads forward slightly and to keep the puppets facing the audience as much as possible. Puppeteers should also try to keep their own bodies from blocking the audience's view of the puppets.

Variation

• Draw simple legs with attached feet on poster board and cut them out. Tuck the top of each leg inside the front edge of the puppet tunic and staple them in place.

Quick-and-Easy Hand Puppet

This is a simple variation of the familiar hand puppet. It can be used to help dramatize most folktales, and will come in handy (no pun intended) if a story character needs to pick up or carry a small object. This puppet may be substituted for the hand-mouth puppets when dramatizing *The Ogre's Staircase* (See Chapter 9).

Preparation Materials

- 3" x 5" index card or postcard
- masking tape
- two paper bowls with plain white bottoms
- sharp scissors
- stapler
- a colorful piece of cloth about 20" square

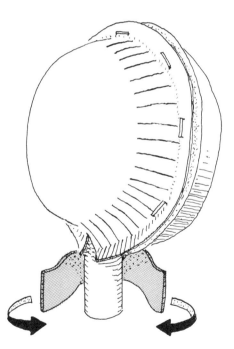

Construction Prep

1. Roll the index card into a snug tube around your index finger. Remove your finger and secure the tube shape with masking tape.

2. Stack one bowl inside the other. Cut a 1" slit through both bowls, starting the cut at any point along the edge of the bowls and running it toward the center. Separate the bowls. Position the card tube inside one of the bowls so the tube's length covers the small slit, and 1" of the tube protrudes beyond the edge of the bowl. Place the second bowl upside down on top of the bowl with the tube, matching the two slit cuts. Press the bowls together gently. Both slits should spread open slightly

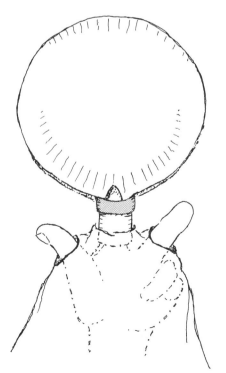

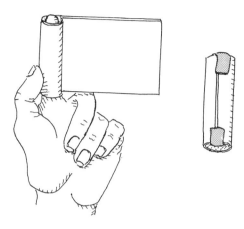

Make a finger-size neck tube from a 3" x 5" card.

(*Left*) The puppet head foundation is constructed of two paper bowls turned to face each other with a finger tube sandwiched in between. Wrap a piece of masking tape around the junction to keep the tube from sliding out.

(*Right*) Show children how the simple puppet parts fit together. They may develop their puppets into characters that perform an original story written by the puppeteers.

around the tube. Staple the bowls together around the edges. Make sure you place a staple on each side of the tube. Secure the tube with a piece of masking tape so it cannot slide in or out of the double bowl. You have just completed the foundation for the puppet's head.

3. Fold the square of cloth in half diagonally, forming a triangle. Cut a dime-size hole at the center point of the fold line. Cut two more dime-size holes along the fold line, one on either side of the original hole, and each about 3" from it. When you open up the cloth, you should see three holes in a row. Pick up the cloth and put your index finger through the central hole, your thumb through one side hole, and your middle finger through the other. This is the puppet's body cloth. Pop the tube neck of the head foundation onto your index finger, and you are looking at a blank-face puppet—just waiting to be created.

If you are planning to work on this puppet with a group of children, prepare several body cloths in a variety of colors and patterns so you can let the children choose.

CHILDREN'S ACTIVITY

Materials

- **prepared puppet head (one per puppet)**
- **felt-tip markers in assorted colors**
- **prepared cloth body (at least one per puppet)**
- **lightweight decorating materials such as yarn, crepe paper streamers, geometric stickers, feathers, curling ribbon, pompoms, cotton balls, scraps of colorful paper**
- **clear plastic tape**
- **white household glue**
- **children's scissors**

Preparing the Work Area

1. Place a puppet head foundation at each child's place at the worktable. Put markers in the center of the table, within easy reach of all.

2. Set aside cloth bodies, decorating materials, tape, glue and children's scissors at a separate area nearby.

Completing the Project

1. Show students how their puppets will fit together by placing a body cloth on your hand, as previously described, and popping a blank puppet head onto your index finger. Point out the neck tube, which marks the bottom of the puppet's head.

2. Using felt-tip markers, children can now draw puppet facial features on one flat surface of the double bowl.

The other flat side can be decorated as the back of the puppet's head.

3. As children finish with the markers, add the decorations, tape, glue and scissors to the worktable supplies.

4. When their puppet heads are completed, the children may choose cloth bodies.

Animating the Puppet

Show the puppeteers how to place the puppets on their hands (body cloths first, then heads). Suggest puppet activities which will encourage children to experiment with puppet manipulation. Can their puppets nod their heads? Shake their heads? Bow? Look at the floor? Read a page from a book?

The thumb and middle finger serve as the puppets' arms. Can students make their puppets clap their hands? Fold their arms across their chests? Pick up a felt-tip marker? Scratch their chins? Pat a neighboring puppet on the back? Give children time to discover other forms of puppet movement.

Students can also experiment with different speaking voices until they find one which suits their puppet. What emotions can the puppeteers communicate using this simple hand puppet?

Variations

• Use the preceding basic construction technique to create puppet head foundations out of plain, white-bottom paper plates or saucers. This will give you a variety of head sizes.

• Foam rubber can often be purchased in different shapes—balls, squares, cylinders—to provide alternative heads for this type of hand puppet. With the help of a utility knife or small sharp scissors, cut two 1" long slits into the bottom of these foam rubber shapes. The slits should cross, forming a small ×. *Safety Note: If you are working with young children, cut the slits yourself. Even with older students, use of utility knives or sharp scissors be supervised closely.*

Put a body cloth on your hand and slide the index finger into the × cut; no cardboard tube is necessary. Children can use felt-tip markers or tempera paint to add features to the foam heads. Attach scraps of cloth, paper and yarn with white glue. Foam rubber heads can also be shaped with scissors, and smaller foam rubber shapes can be glued on to produce a wide variety of animal puppets.

• In place of colored cloth, prepare puppet bodies out of white cotton cloth. Let students provide their own designs and patterns with colored felt-tip markers or vegetable prints with tempera paints.

Enchanting Fairy

A zephyr of flowing garments and dazzling sequins, this fanciful marionette floats across the room to foil the terrible ogre's plot (See *The Ogre's Staircase* in Chapter 9).

PAVING THE WAY

Preparation Materials

- two flat wooden control rods one 22" long, one 14" long (You can saw a wooden yardstick in two at the 22" mark.)
- white household glue
- masking tape
- two sturdy, rigid paper plates with plain white bottoms
- stapler
- one square yard of lightweight colorful cloth
- clear plastic tape
- six pipe cleaners (the glittery kind, if you have them)
- scissors
- monofilament (fishing line) or strong black thread
- measuring tape

Construction Prep

1. Center the 22" rod over one end of the 14" rod, forming a T shape. Glue the rods together in this position. Wrap a little masking tape diagonally around the junction of the two rods in both directions to reinforce the joint. The tape will keep the rods together while the glue is drying.

2. Set one of the plates on a table in a right-side up position. Turn the second plate upside down, and place it on top of the first plate, matching the edges. (The plate bottoms should face away from each other, forming the outside surfaces.) Staple the plates together around the edges; this plump double plate will become the fairy's head.

3. Fold the square yard of cloth in half diagonally, forming a large triangle. Tuck an edge of the double plate under the cloth at the center point of the fold line. Staple the cloth to the double plate edge at this point. Run the cloth fold along the plate edges for 3" on both sides of the central staple. Staple the cloth to the plate edge at both these points. (This three-point attachment should prevent the puppet's head from spinning around on its body.) Gather a small wad of cloth at one end of the diagonal fold line, and wrap a band of clear plastic tape around the bunched cloth; this will form one of the puppet's wrists. Repeat this process at the other end of the fold line.

4. Cut all the pipe cleaners in half.

5. Tie one end of the monofilament or thread around one end of the longer (22") control rod. If you use monofilament, add extra loops to your knots to prevent the line from sliding out of its knots. Maneuver the tied line to the very end of the 22" rod, and secure it with a piece of masking tape. Allow the line to dangle down from the rod for a length of 24"; cut off excess line. Repeat this procedure with another piece of line at the other end of the 22" control rod. Tie a third piece of line around the 14" rod near the point where it is glued to the longer rod; secure with masking tape. Let this line hang down for a length of only 8" and cut off the excess line. Your T-shape control rod should now have three dangling strings.

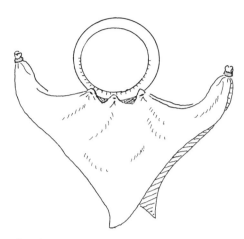

The cloth body is attached to the head at three points. The wrist bunches are located at the ends of the fold line.

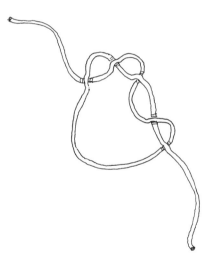

Use extra loops and twists when tying monofilament, or your knots will spring apart when you turn your back on them.

Materials

- **prepared puppet head with attached cloth body (one per puppet)**
- **felt-tip markers in assorted colors**
- **decorations such as sequins, colorful reflective paper, glitter glue, tinsel, glittering tree garlands, aluminum foil, crepe paper streamers, curling ribbon**
- **white household glue**
- **children's scissors**
- **twelve pipe cleaner halves (twelve halves per puppet)**
- **clear plastic tape**
- **T-shape control rod with three dangling strings (one per puppet)**

Preparing the Work Area

1. Place a puppet head at each child's work space so that the flat side with the cloth stapled to it is facing up. (This will become the puppet's face.) The cloth body can be scrunched up loosely so it doesn't get in the way. Position markers, glue, scissors and decorations within easy reach.

2. Set aside control rods, tape and pipe cleaners in a convenient location.

Completing the Project

1. Hold up one of the double plate heads and show the children how the puppet's body hangs down from it. Have students decorate one flat side of their puppet heads as the fairy's face, and the other as the back of its head. Point out the materials available for developing the puppets, then step back and watch the fairies evolve.

2. Once children have completed their puppet heads, give each of them ten pipe cleaner halves. Students can tape or twist these together to form two long-fingered hands for the fairy. They should have two extra pipe cleaner halves left after the hands are made. Have each student place the heel of one hand on a wrist bunch, then wrap an extra pipe cleaner half tightly around the area where wrist and hand overlap. Students should repeat the process for the second hand. Make sure the hands are attached firmly; reinforce with clear plastic tape if necessary.

3. Now it's time to attach each fairy to a control rod. Have a child grasp the control rod at the base of the T and hold it out in front, with the strings dangling down. Staple the free end of the short central string to the top edge of the plate head. (The puppet should be facing forward—like the puppeteer.) Make sure that the control string is attached securely and will not pull loose. You may need to double the end of the string back on itself and staple again, tie a knot in the end, or reinforce your staple attachment with a piece of clear plastic tape. Secure the longer strings to the puppet's wrists.

The marionette is attached to three control strings.

Animating the Puppet

The puppeteer holds the puppet out in front while holding the control rod near the base of the T, although a small puppeteer may do better to hold the rod at a point halfway along its length. When the crosspiece (crossbar of the T) is rocked, the fairy's hands will rise and fall alternately. The puppeteer can move the puppet around the room while experimenting with different styles—a gentle undulating float, a swoop, a rocking sashay. Spell-casting movements can be developed. If the puppeteer wants to raise one fairy's hand without affecting the other, simply pull up on that hand's control string.

Variations

• Construct lightweight magic wands out of pipe cleaners, paper and glitter. The fairies can clasp this most useful of tools in their flexible fingers.

• Children can, of course, develop this marionette into many other story characters. The loose floating movement of this puppet might conjure up the image of a ghost, goddess, or character from a dream.

Adaptable Multi-Puppet

If you are working with a small group of children and your story calls for a cast of thousands, the multi-puppet can help you out. With this puppet, one child can represent a group of dancing villagers, an army on the march, a thundering herd of zebras or a flock of birds. The possibilities are limitless; just don't tell the actors union.

PAVING THE WAY

Preparation Materials

- plastic drop cloth
- two 22" x 28" sheets of poster board
- white household glue
- paintbrush (2" or 3" wide works best)

Construction Prep

1. Spread out the drop cloth and lay one of the pieces of poster board on top of it. Coat the entire top side of the poster board with a thin layer of white glue.

2. Lay the other piece of poster board on top of this gluey surface, match the edges, and press them together. Weight the surface with books or other heavy objects until the glue is dry.

CHILDREN'S ACTIVITY

Materials

- drop cloth or newspapers
- prepared double sheet of poster board
- construction paper in assorted colors
- white household glue
- children's scissors
- felt-tip markers in assorted colors
- colorful wrapping paper (optional)
- duct tape
- two pipe cleaners

Preparing the Work Area

1. Spread a drop cloth or newspapers over the floor or table work space. Lay the doubled poster board on the drop cloth and put the construction paper, glue, children's scissors, felt-tip markers and wrapping paper (if available) within easy reach.

2. Set aside the duct tape and pipe cleaners for later use.

Completing the Project

1. Invite one child into the work space. Designate one edge of the poster board to be the top. Have the child draw figures on construction paper. When finished, cut the figures cut out and glue them to the doubled poster board, which serves as a supportive backing. Encourage the puppeteer to cover most of the poster board surface with figures. The visual effect will be more interesting if the figures overlap somewhat. Extend the figures near the edges of the poster board a little beyond the edges (a head here, a leg there) to create a dynamic outline. Encourage the child to use only small dabs of glue.

2. Once the glue is dry, carefully turn the poster board over and attach two pipe cleaner handles to the central area of its backside. Position these handles parallel to the side edges of the poster board, about a child's body width apart. Use duct tape to attach the ends of the pipe cleaners securely to the poster board; leave a little arching slack at the middle of each pipe cleaner, so it can be grasped easily.

Pipe cleaner handles are attached to the back of the multi-puppet.

Animating the Puppet

With a handle in each hand, the puppeteer can hold this puppet in front of his or her body and march, dance or fly the pictured characters into view. Give the child time to practice different movements and approaches until the desired effect is gained. Encourage the puppeteer to try little bounces, slow undulations, rocking, and tilting movements. This puppet's effect can be enhanced if other children help supply vocals and other sound effects.

Variations

• Attach a lightweight cloth to the back of the bottom edge of the multi-puppet. This will hang down to conceal the legs of the puppeteer.

• If you want the multi-puppet to appear above a curtain, attach a T-shape control rod to the puppet's back with glue and masking tape. Glue the crossbar of the T to the top back of the poster board to keep the poster board from folding in on itself.

• If a stiffer or larger multi-puppet backing is desired, use a sheet of heavy-duty cardboard. Use a utility knife to cut it to the desired size.

• If your multi-puppet represents a flock of birds, cut out a single paper wing for each bird. Glue one end of each wing to each bird on the multi-puppet. The free ends of the wings should reach out horizontally from the poster board. When the multi-puppet is raised and lowered, the wings will flap, adding movement and dimension to the puppet.

• Enliven a multi-puppet further by adding moveable legs to the figures in the bottom row. When the children draw the construction paper figures, instruct them to draw a few without legs. Glue these figures to the bottom section of the poster board so that their hips are near the bottom edge. Draw legs separately on thin cardboard or poster board. Cut out the legs and attach them to the multi-puppet with paper fasteners, then watch them kick and jiggle about when the puppet is moved. For extra animation, cut each leg into two sections and attach the upper leg to its lower part with an additional paper fastener. If you jiggle this type of hinged multi-puppet in the air or tap the feet of the hinged legs gently on a tabletop, the legs will flex and leap with delightful abandon.

• Direct a group of children to work together to create this puppet. After it is completed, one child can operate it during the performance while the other artists provide the sound effects—hoof beats, bird songs, cheering voices, or whatever is appropriate to the pictured figures.

This multi-puppet features a flock of flying birds with wings that flap up and down. It could just as easily be developed to represent a thundering herd of zebras or a marching band of village musicians.

THREE

Large Puppets

Is it Bigger Than a Bread Box?

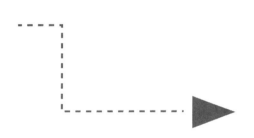

Large puppets add an exciting dimension to any puppet show or parade. Let's face it, a squeaky pocket-size ogre does not have the same visceral effect on the audience as one looming three feet over their heads. Ogres, after all, are not known for their subtlety. Even those children who think puppets are kid stuff will be unable to resist the lure of the large puppet.

Many of the puppets described in this chapter are designed to be created and animated by a team of children, developing the cooperative skills of these puppeteers. The puppet-making instructions are designed to help you get started. Feel free to experiment and improvise.

High-Flying Bird

Buoyed by air pressure and activated by a simple up-and-down movement of the control rod, the flexible wings of this puppet ply the air gracefully. Watching a flock of these large, colorful birds as they swoop lazily across a room provides a visual caress for any audience.

These puppets are very popular with children in dramatizations and parades.

PAVING THE WAY

Preparation Materials

- pencil
- two full sheets (22" x 28") of white poster board
- scissors
- 2' or 3' long, sturdy, flat, wooden control rod
- white glue and a glue brush
- masking tape
- twenty spring-type clothespins
- stapler (pliers-type works best)
- yardstick

Construction Prep

1. Fold one of the sheets of poster board in half, matching the short edges. You should end up with a doubled 22" x 14" rectangle of poster board. With a pencil, draw a wingless bird body on one side of the doubled poster board. No fancy artwork is required here! Just draw a large oblong body, then add a smaller roundish shape on one end for the bird's head and an overlapping triangle for the tail. Make the whole bird as long as the poster board will allow, and incorporate the outer edge of the bird's back, head and tail into the fold line.

2. Cut out the bird's outline with your scissors, cutting through both layers of poster board at once. *Do not*

Draw the bird body using simple shapes; children will elaborate on the design later. Incorporate the fold line into the outline of the bird's head, back and tail.

cut the fold line where it is incorporated into the outline of your bird body. You should end up with a double bird body joined in three places along the fold line.

3. Attach a control rod to the inside of the double bird's midsection with white glue. The top of the control rod should reach about three-quarters of

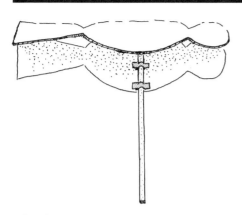

Glue the control rod to the inside of the double bird body, with the rod extending about three-quarters of the way into the puppet. Reinforce the control rod with tape.

the way up the bird's body. (Do not extend the rod all the way up to the top of the bird's back, because you will have to staple a pair of wings to this area later on.) Most of the length of the control rod will extend out from the bottom of the bird's midsection.

Reinforce the rod attachment with a few strips of masking tape. Spread some glue all along the inside of the bird's body. Press the matching poster board bird bodies together and clamp them along the edges with spring-type clothespins. Allow the glue to dry undisturbed for at least thirty minutes. After you remove the clothespins, stabilize the control rod by stapling through both layers of poster board at a point 1" above the top of the control rod and 1" out from both sides of the rod where it exits the bird's body.

4. Cut out a pair of matching wings from the remaining sheet of poster board. Each wing should be a long rectangular shape with one end somewhat rounded to form the wing tip. In order to be efficient flappers, these wings need to be big enough to catch air but not so heavy that they droop sadly at the bird's sides. Design the wings in any shape that pleases your eye as long as each wing is about 7" wide and 15" to 21" long.

CHILDREN'S ACTIVITY

Materials

- prepared bird body with attached rod (one per puppet)
- duct tape
- feathers
- construction paper in assorted colors (Make sure you have plenty of yellow and orange.)
- children's scissors
- oil pastels in assorted colors
- clear plastic tape
- white household glue
- pair of poster board wings (one per puppet)
- crayons in assorted colors
- stapler (pliers-type, if you have it)

Preparing the Work Area

1. Attach the rod of the prepared bird body to a chair back or table leg with duct tape, placing the bird in an upright position. This will enable the child to work on both sides at once.

2. Keep the feathers, construction paper, children's scissors, oil pastels, clear plastic tape and glue handy nearby.

3. Set up a separate work area with the prepared wings and the crayons. Store the stapler nearby.

Completing the Project

1. Children can use oil pastels to color their birds in any style, pattern or color combination they wish. Remind them that the birds have two sides to decorate. Encourage students to experiment with color and design. Instead of coloring their birds with solid coats of color, they might consider using stripes or speckles, or maybe geometric designs which simulate feathers. Point out the construction paper and scissors, and let children know they can use these materials to make feet, beaks and eyes for their birds. Feathers can be added to a bird's tail or head for added visual interest.

56

Tell students not to worry about the wings at this point, as they will be working on these later.

2. When children have finished with the birds' bodies, they can move to the separate work area to decorate the poster board wings with crayons. Encourage them to experiment with lines and shapes which give the impression of feathers. For added effect, scissors can be used to remove small triangles of poster board from the rounded tips of the wings; the remaining points will resemble the tips of the primary feathers. *Feathers and other decorations should not be glued or taped to the wings, or they may become too cumbersome to flap properly.*

3. When the decorations are complete, it's time to attach the wings. Ask the children to hold one wing on each side of their bird's upper back, with most of the wing's surface held above the bird's body and the wing tips pointing toward the ceiling. The 7" straight edge of each wing should overlap the bird's upper back by 1" or 2".

Staple both wings to the top of the bird's back by reaching in with your stapler from either side of the wings and securing both corners of the straight 7" wing ends and as far along this edge as you can. You will probably not be able to place a staple in the centermost area of the 7" straight wing edge.

Allow the wings to fall open loosely. You may need to gently press the wings open with your hand until they are

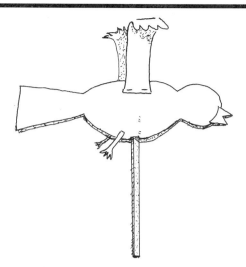

Attach the wings to the top of the bird body.

more or less horizontal to the floor. *Do not put a permanent crease in the wings, or they will lack springiness and hang like wilted lettuce leaves.*

4. Release the completed bird puppets from their duct tape restraints.

Animating the Puppet

Once their wings are reaching out from the sides, the puppets will offer resistance to the air. Advise children to hold their puppet control rods vertically straight while moving the puppets slowly up and down and watch the birds flap gracefully above their heads. Once students have mastered this, they can practice flying their puppets around the room. Encourage children to experiment with puppet movement to find the best effects.

Variations

• With a few minor changes, construct a bat puppet. Use black poster board when making the double body foundation, add a nose bulge to the round head shape, and eliminate the tail. Then attach the control rod. Presto—you'll have a pig on a stick. But never fear! Have children add eyes and facial features by cutting them from reflective paper or drawing them on with glitter glue. Attach construction paper ears to the top of the head and feet to the bottom of the body near the back. Make the wings from black poster board, sizing them an inch or two wider than the bird's wings, and let the children cut shallow scallops into the black edges. The pig on a stick is now transformed into a *bona fide* bat swooping darkly through the air. A great addition to your Halloween parade.

• But don't stop there! With a few changes in body shape, this puppet could easily be developed into a pterodactyl, winged dragon or high-flying Pegasus.

• Use tempera paints or water-soluble crayons to color the bird bodies. You will have to allow the paint to dry before the paper feet and beaks can be attached. The children can make these paper bird parts and decorate the bird wings with crayons while the paint dries.

Industrious Horse

This rod puppet comes in handy in stories featuring people on horseback. It can easily be adapted into a two-person puppet. And it fairly cries out for galloping sound effects—so dust off those coconut shells!

Preparation Materials

- a clear picture of a side view of a horse's head (a good photocopy would be fine)
- tracing paper
- stapler
- black felt-tip marker
- full sheet of white poster board 22" x 28" or larger (one per puppet)

Construction Prep

1. Place tracing paper over the horse-head picture and staple them together along one edge.

2. Use the black felt-tip marker to trace the basic shapes found in the picture of the horse head: a circular shape around the upper head, an oval over the long nose and a trapezoid around the neck.

3. Fold the poster board in half by bringing the short edges together.

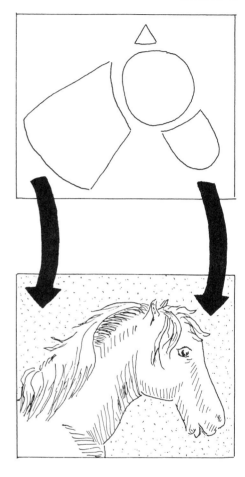

(Right): Superimpose the prepared tracing paper over the picture to demonstrate the simple shapes that make up a horse's head. This type of visual aide can help children overcome drawing blocks.

CHILDREN'S ACTIVITY

Materials

- tracing-paper horse head drawing guide
- folded poster board (one per puppet)
- pencil
- children's scissors

- crayons or oil pastels in assorted colors
- construction paper in assorted colors
- white household glue

- sturdy, smooth, flat wooden control rod approximately 3' long, such as a wooden yardstick (one per puppet)
- stapler
- crepe paper streamers, ribbon, yarn

Preparing the Work Area

1. Place a folded sheet of poster board, a pencil and scissors at each child's work place. Keep the tracing-paper horse head drawing guide near at hand.

2. Set aside other materials nearby for later use.

Completing the Project

1. With the tracing paper shape guide flipped out of the way, show students the picture of the horse head and ask them if they can find different shapes which fit together to form the image. Flip the tracing paper back over the picture and show students the shape guide. Ask them to compare how big or small the shapes are in relation to one another. Tell children to keep these observations in mind while they draw a large side view of a horse head on folded poster board. Caution them to use the pencil lightly in case they want to make any alternations. *The top edge of their horse's neck should run along the fold line.* Ask them to draw the head and neck as large as the poster board will allow. They can use your shape guide as a drawing aid, or they can invent their own shapes to aid them in drawing their horse-head profiles. Tell children not to add ears to their drawings, as they will be making sets of paper ears later.

2. When their drawings are complete, students can cut out their horse

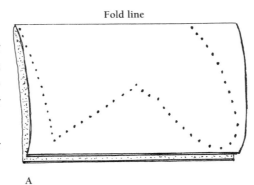

Fold line

A

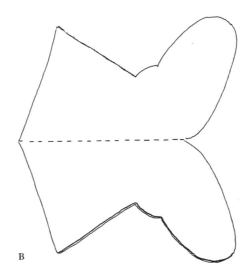

B

Incorporate the poster board fold line into the horse's neckline. After the double head is cut out, open it up for decorating before refolding it and attaching it to the control rod.

heads, cutting through both layers of poster board at once to produce two matching horse heads joined at the fold line. *Make sure children understand not to cut along the fold line.*

3. Unfold each horse head and place the double head flat on the table so both outside surfaces can be worked on at once. Make the crayons or oil pastels, construction paper and glue available for the children to add color and facial features to their horse heads. Cut out and glue on construction paper ears and eyelashes. Tell students they will have a chance to add a mane later.

4. When children have finished, help them attach control rods to their horse heads. Have each of them support the rod while you drape the horse's head and neck over one end of it. The rod should run along the inside of the folded top edge of the horse's neck. Secure the head to the control rod with the stapler, and staple the two head sections together along their matching edges.

5. For the flowing mane, have children cut crepe paper streamers, ribbon or yarn into convenient lengths and glue them onto the horses' necks. For a curly, bouncy mane, cut construction paper into strips and curl them by wrapping them around a pencil.

Animating the Puppet

The child operating this puppet simply rides the rod puppet like a hobbyhorse. The rod can also be handheld to make the horse appear as a puppet head from the top or side of a stage curtain.

Variations

• The Industrious Horse is at its most appealing when it is converted into a two-person puppet. You will need a piece of cloth large enough to cover all but the legs of two children bent forward at the waist and standing one-behind-the-other; 2 yards x 1 1/2 yards should do the trick. Find the middle spot of one of the shorter edges of the cloth and use a piece of twine or duct tape to secure it firmly to the control rod just below the poster board head.

Construct a tail by cutting several strands of string, twine, yarn or crepe paper streamers into 2' lengths. Lay the strands side by side. Tie them together at one end, and attach the knot to the cloth body with a safety pin or stapler.

If desired, the children could create a set of four poster board horse legs with black construction paper hooves to be stapled to the cloth body. Add some stripes to transform the horse into a prancing zebra.

The child in the back of the horse can hit together two plastic yogurt containers or coconut shell halves to provide a clip-clop sound effect. The two puppeteers may want to exchange positions once in a while to see how the other half lives.

Operating the Two-Person Horse Puppet

The child in front bends forward at the waist while holding onto the rod of the horse head. The child in the rear also bends forward, with one hand on each hip of the child standing in front. The cloth body is draped over both of them. The child in front maneuvers the horse's head. Give the puppeteers time to practice moving together before their puppet appears in a show.

Add a large piece of cloth and a second puppeteer to create this lumpy but lovable steed. The child who is holding up the rear can hit the open ends of two plastic cups together to produce the pleasant clip clop of horse hooves.

Sinuous Dragon

This mythical creature is the perfect puppet for a group project, requiring four to twelve children for its construction and operation. The dragon is guaranteed to create a dramatic stir in your puppet show; a chorus of "oohs" and "aahs" will accompany its winding promenade along your parade route.

PAVING THE WAY

Preparation Materials

- two pieces of heavyweight cardboard (roughly 30" x 35" and 25" x 32")
- yardstick
- pencil
- cutting board or old piece of carpet
- utility knife
- white household glue
- two sturdy, flat wooden control rods (See "Materials Guide" in Chapter 1)
- masking tape
- stapler (pliers-type works best)
- mixture of two parts liquid white tempera paint to one part white household glue, drop cloth, 1" or 2" paintbrush (optional)

- scissors
- white poster board
- medium-size nail or Phillips screwdriver with a narrow shaft
- large paper fastener (1 1/2" long works well)
- duct tape
- a rubber band about 1/16" x 1/8" x 8"
- stapler (pliers-type works best)

Construction Prep

1. Draw a dragon's tail roughly 30" long and 10" to 12" tall on the smaller piece of sturdy cardboard. You may draw one similar to the illustration, design one in your own style, or simply draw a large, spiny triangle.

2. Draw a dragon's head on the larger piece of cardboard; do not include the dragon's lower jaw in this drawing, but allow space for it on the cardboard. The head should be about 33" long and 22" at its highest point.

Remember, we are talking about a mythical animal here, so anything goes, but use the illustration as a rough guide if you like. Add toothy projections to the bottom of the snout and

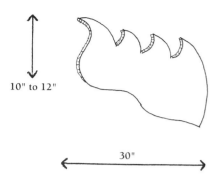

10" to 12"

30"

This is one example of a design for the dragon's tail. Feel free to elaborate or simplify.

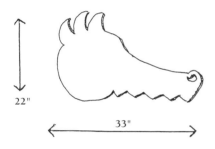

22"

33"

Draw a large, dramatic dragon head. The lower jaw will be drawn later as a separate and movable piece.

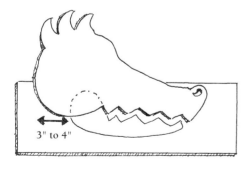

3" to 4"

Draw the lower jaw on a leftover section of cardboard. This should include a half-circle pivotal area at the top back of the lower jaw piece.

some reptilian spikes to the head. (Dragons are prickly creatures.)

3. Lay the cardboard with the dragon head on a piece of old carpet, on a cutting board or outside on the grass, and cut out the dragon's head with a utility knife. Put the head and the leftover cardboard aside for a moment and cut out the dragon's tail.

Place the cut-out dragon head on top of the leftover cardboard, with the cheek and jaw of the head overlapping the top 6" to 8" of the cardboard underneath it. Draw a toothy lower jaw on the bottom piece of cardboard 3" to 4" shorter than the upper head piece at the back of the head. Lift off the upper dragon head and draw a half circle on top of the lower jaw at the back end. This will give you an overlapping area of cardboard to use later for hinging the lower jaw to the rest of the dragon's head. Cut out the lower jaw with the utility knife.

4. Lay the upper part of the dragon's head and the tail down on the floor, and glue a wooden control rod to each. Make sure the rod on the dragon's head is attached near the back edge of the head so that it will not interfere with the lower jaw movement. Reinforce with masking tape and allow the glue to dry. Add reinforcing staples if the head-rod connection seems shaky.

5. Optional step: You may choose to add a base coat of white glue and tempera paint to the cardboard dragon head and tail. This will make the pieces stronger and cover up any logos

Attach the control rods to the dragon's head and tail with glue and masking tape.

on the cardboard. Also, the oil pastel or paint colors the children use to decorate the pieces will appear brighter and more colorful. If you plan on having children use sheets of brightly colored paper to cover the dragon's head and tail, skip this step.

Spread an old shower curtain or other drop cloth on the floor. Lay the dragon's head, tail and lower jaw on the drop cloth and brush on a thin coat of the paint-glue mixture. Allow to dry. Flip each piece over and coat its other side with the same mixture. Allow to dry.

6. Cut the sheet of white poster board into eight equal pieces, each roughly 11" x 7". You will need one of these pieces for every child who is to be part of the dragon's body, so cut another poster board into sections if needed. (The children operating the dragon's head and tail will not need one.)

7. Lay the dragon's upper head on a flat surface, and place the lower jaw piece on top of it in such a way that they overlap in the cheek area. The

63

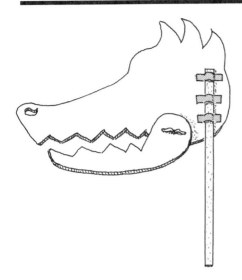

Secure the dragon's lower jaw to the head with a paper fastener.

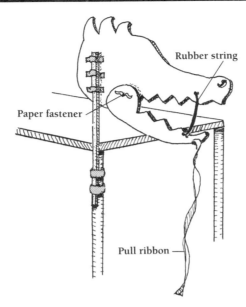

Paper fastener

Rubber string

Pull ribbon

Temporarily secure the puppet's control rod to a chair back or a table leg in such a way that the lower jaw can be opened and closed freely. Attach and adjust the rubber band to the jaw.

upper head with its rod should extend 3" or 4" beyond the lower jaw at the back. Place the point of your nail or screwdriver somewhere in the center of the overlap area and poke a hole through both pieces of cardboard. Thread a large paper fastener through this hole and spread open its ends, joining the two head pieces together. You should now be able to move the lower jaw freely so that the dragon's mouth can open and close.

8. Using duct tape, attach the dragon's head control rod to a chair or table leg in such a way that the head is upright the jaw can open and close freely, and both sides of the head can be easily reached by the child who is to decorate it. Make a single cut in the rubber band to create a rubber string. Staple one end of this rubber string to the dragon's upper jaw near the outer end of the snout. Make sure that the string cannot be pulled out from under the staple. Close the dragon's teeth together. Staple the dangling part of the rubber string to the lower jaw, experimenting a little with the string's tension and placement. Ideally the rubber string should be attached in such a way that it provides enough tension to hold the upper and lower jaws loosely together but allows enough elasticity for the dragon's mouth to open in a toothy gape when you pull down on the outer tip of its lower jaw. Make sure that the rubber string is not going to pull loose at the ends. (Knot the ends of the rubber string or tie them around the staples.) Cut off any surplus string.

CHILDREN'S ACTIVITY

Materials

- duct tape
- prepared dragon head and tail
- oil pastels in a variety of colors
- sheets of tissue paper and wrapping paper in a variety of colors

- doodads, gegaws and gimcracks to decorate the dragon's head and tail (ribbons, tissue paper, glitter, garlands, tinsel, etc.)
- white household glue
- clear plastic tape

- prepared 11" x 7" sections of white poster board and a large or small craft stick control rod
- several felt-tip markers
- children's scissors
- stapler (pliers-type, if you have it)

- 11" x 7" pieces of aluminum foil or metallic wrapping paper
- one long, lightweight piece of colorful cloth approximately 1 1/2 yards wide, or several shorter pieces sewn together to make one long piece (Allow 3' of length for the child at the dragon's head, 2' for each child in the dragon's body and 3' for the child holding the dragon's tail.)
- crepe paper streamers, curling ribbon, aluminum foil, colorful plastic surveyor's ribbon or tinsel
- one backpack (child-size if available)
- 5' piece of ribbon, yarn or string

Preparing the Work Area

1. As you did with the dragon's head, use duct tape to attach the dragon's tail rod to a chair back or table leg so that both sides of the tail can be easily reached by the child who is to decorate it. Set out the oil pastels, tissue paper, wrapping paper and glue. Place the other decorative materials nearby with the clear plastic tape.

2. Set up a work area at a table or on the floor for the children who will be making the dragon's claws. Each child should have one of the 11" x 7" pieces of poster board, a large or small craft stick, a felt-tip marker and a pair of scissors. Make sure that the work area also has glue, a stapler and enough aluminum foil or metallic wrapping paper to cover all of the dragon's feet.

3. Spread the long piece of fabric out on the floor. Place the crepe paper, ribbons, foil, tinsel, children's scissors and clear plastic tape nearby.

4. Set aside the backpack and 5' ribbon, yarn or string for later use.

Completing the Project

1. The children who will operate the dragon's head and tail may color these parts in whatever combination and design style they like. They might cover them with colorful tissue and wrapping papers using large, flat shapes or overlapping smaller pieces to form scales. Remind students to use small dabs of glue to attach the paper pieces to the dragon. They might prefer to cover large areas with color using oil pastels. If so, peel the paper off the pastel sticks and use the sides to apply colors more efficiently. Students might choose to use a combination of techniques. Remind them that the head and tail have two sides to decorate. Demonstrate the dragon's jaw movement to the child decorating the dragon's head, and caution the student to avoid adding any decorations which would interfere with the free movement of the jaw. The dragon will also need a suitably impressive eye on each side of its head.

Once these two children have provided the head and tail background color and the dragon's facial features, they can attach streamers and other deco-

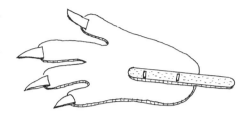

A craft stick acts as a control rod for each dragon foot.

rations to the pieces to create a sense of dynamic flowing movement.

2. Direct the children who will play the part of the dragon's body to the dragon-claw work area. Encourage them to draw their own conception of a dragon's foot on a piece of 11" x 7" poster board, making it as large as possible. Once children have designed the feet, they can cut them out with scissors. Glue a piece of decorating paper or foil to one side of each foot, and cut away the excess paper. Pointed paper claws in a contrasting color can be glued onto the tip of each dragon toe, if desired. Flip each completed foot over and staple a craft stick control rod to its undecorated side. Two or three inches of this control rod should extend out from the dragon's heel, to provide a handle. Reinforce with tape, if needed.

3. While the glue is drying, children can move to the outspread cloth which is to be the dragon's body. Have them cut 1' long strips of crepe paper streamers, curling ribbon or aluminum foil. Attach one end of each strip to the long piece of cloth with clear plastic tape. Allow the rest of each strip to dangle freely. These lightweight strips will ripple and dance about when the dragon moves.

4. When all of the decorations are complete, remove the duct tape holding the dragon's head and tail to the supporting table or chair. Place the head at one end of the cloth body and the tail at the other. Ask a child to hold the head upright with its rod resting on the floor. Drape one of the 1 1/2-yard-wide edges of the cloth over the back edge of the dragon head so that it hangs down fairly evenly on both sides. Use several staples to secure the cloth to the head in this position. Repeat this process at the other end of the cloth, attaching the front forward edge of the dragon tail to the center of the other 1 1/2-yard edge of the cloth. Use several staples, making sure each attachment is secure.

5. Tie one end of the 5' ribbon around the frontmost section of the dragon's lower jaw, or punch a small hole there and thread the string through. By gently pulling and releasing pressure on this ribbon, the child controlling the puppet's head can open and close the dragon's mouth.

Animating the Puppet

The child who operates the head of the dragon should wear the backpack in front of his or her chest. When the bottom end of the control rod is placed in the backpack, the backpack will help support the weight of the dragon's head. This child can use one hand to steady the control rod, leaving the other hand free to pull the string which operates the dragon's mouth. If the child prefers to have both hands on the control rod, the next child in line can operate the string controlling the dragon's mouth.

The children who form the dragon's body should stand in line under the cloth, behind the child who holds the dragon head. They should each put one hand on the shoulder of the person standing in front of them to coordinate movements. If students keep these connecting arms straight and stiff, their arms will also act as spacers. With their free hands they can hold the rods of their dragon claws. Make sure the claws poke out from under the cloth so they can be seen. The dragon will look more capable if it has some claws on each side of its body. The children can bend forward at the waist or stand upright, depending on preference for smooth or lumpy dragons.

The child controlling the dragon's tail should stand at the end of the line, holding the control rod in both hands. A few dramatic sweeps or wags of the tail will increase the dragon's dramatic effect.

Before the dragon begins to move, remind puppeteers that their dragon will move more impressively if they all work together. Each person should follow the movements of the person immediately in front. (Otherwise, the dragon may look like it's being drawn and quartered.)

The children will have worked hard to get this far, so encourage them to enjoy themselves as they experiment with different types of movement. The dragon can wind through the area in slow, lazy curves or advance in choppy foot-waving menace. Ask the children to suggest other movements they think might look interesting. The dragon's mouth can be opened and closed to speak, yawn or show off its teeth.

A dragon such as this deserves satisfying sound effects. A cymbal, gong or large drum would be great! If these are not available, try some of the alternatives suggested in Chapter 8. Since puppeteers will have their hands full, you are the logical choice for sound-effects operator. You will probably find this a very enjoyable activity—you may have to be forcibly separated from your drumstick at the end of the performance.

Variations

• Have the children operating this puppet provide some of their own sound effects. Give them some pipe cleaners and bells (the small, jingly kind with the little metal loop). Thread a few bells onto each pipe cleaner. When these pipe cleaners are worn around the puppeteer's ankles, they will signal the dragon's approach with each step.

• This puppet can be used to great effect by two wheelchair-bound students and their classmates. Duct-tape the dragon's head control rod to one wheelchair and the tail rod to the other. When the dragon moves forward across the room, it will glide so smoothly—it will seem to be flying.

• Brightly decorate the head and tail of the dragon with tempera paints or water-soluble crayons instead of oil pastels and tissue paper. If you choose this option, you will have to allow time for the paint to dry before adding decorations. An electric hair drier can shorten the drying time.

Shortcut

• Skip the movable jaw option and draw a simple one-piece dragon head. Attach the control rod and let children use oil pastels and colorful paper to decorate the head.

Stately Giraffe

This two-person puppet is lanky, loose-limbed and brightly colored. Its soft foam head perched atop a lengthy tubular neck can help you sweep the dust balls off the ceiling between performances.

Once you have prepared the foundation work for this puppet ("Paving the Way"), allow children two work sessions to complete the puppet. In the first session students will paint parts of the giraffe body. After the paint has dried, they can complete the decoration and development of the puppet in the second session. Allow one hour for each work session and plan for a minimum of one overnight between the two sessions for the paint to dry. If this creates a scheduling problem, check out the shortcut suggestion at the end of the "Variations" section (page 71).

Preparation Materials

- large cardboard box (washing machine or refrigerator size) or large piece of sturdy cardboard, roughly 58" x 48"
- utility or steak knife
- drop cloth (An old sheet will do.)
- cutting board
- piece of foam rubber at least 8" wide, 12" long and 3" or 4" thick (If foam rubber is not available, see "Variations" at the end of the instructions to substitute a paper bag.)
- orange felt-tip marker
- sturdy cardboard tube 1 1/2" to 2" in diameter and 4' or 5' long
- two cardboard tubes from bathroom tissue or one paper towel tube cut in half
- white household glue
- 22" x 28" sheet of orange poster board (white will work if orange is unobtainable)
- scissors
- yardstick

Construction Prep

1. If you managed to get your hands on a large cardboard box (available for the asking at most large appliance stores), cut off its top and bottom with a utility or steak knife. Stand the box on one of its open ends and make a vertical cut from top to bottom along one of the corner edge fold lines. You should now have a large piece of cardboard with four panels. Cut along the entire length of the middle fold line. You should now have two large pieces of cardboard, each with a fold running down its center or, more importantly, two potential giraffe bodies. Put the extra piece in storage—you never know when you might need another giraffe body.

If you are starting with a plain large flat piece of cardboard, you will need to make your own fold. Fold the cardboard in half so you have one fold running lengthwise. This activity is a little like wrestling with a giant tortilla, so be firm and resolute!

2. Open up the folded cardboard and round off all four corners with the utility knife so that the cardboard is now roughly an oval-shape giraffe body.

3. Cover a table with a drop cloth and place a cutting board on top. Slap that foam rubber onto the cutting board and use the orange felt-tip marker to draw an outline of the front view of a giraffe head on it. Use a book or magazine picture of a giraffe head as a

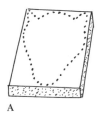 

Snip away at the foam rubber until it resembles a giraffe head.

reference. A simplified giraffe head might bear a striking resemblance to a light bulb. Feel free to improve on this design, but don't forget to include two triangular ears.

Cut out the giraffe head with the utility knife, using short, repetitive stroking movements as you cut down through the foam rubber.

4. Place one end of the long cardboard tube perpendicular against the back of the giraffe head so that it is roughly centered in the upper half of the head. With the orange felt-tip marker, draw a circle on the head around the end of the tube or stick, marking this area as the place where the neck tube will be attached.

Using the orange circle as your guide, cut straight down into the back of the giraffe head with small controlled strokes of the utility knife. *Be careful not to cut all the way through the head!* Make the cuts about 2" deep near the bottom of the circle and taper them off gradually to only 1" deep near the top

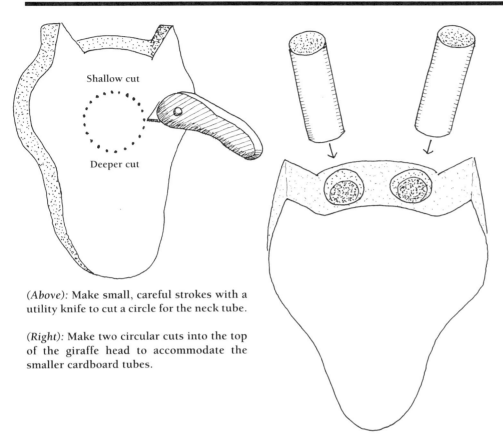

(*Above*): Make small, careful strokes with a utility knife to cut a circle for the neck tube.

(*Right*): Make two circular cuts into the top of the giraffe head to accommodate the smaller cardboard tubes.

side of one end of the large cardboard tube. Push the glue-covered tube end firmly into the circular cut in the back of the giraffe head using a twisting motion, with the foam circle plug inside the tube. The tube should slide in more deeply at the bottom (deeper) half of the cut so that the head joins the neck tube at a 45-degree angle. Prop the tube and head assembly over a chair back, and allow the glue to dry overnight.

7. Fold the poster board in half lengthwise. Open it up and cut along the fold line with scissors. Store one piece for future projects, and fold the remaining piece in half lengthwise again. Open it up and cut along the fold line. Using a yardstick, draw a diagonal line to bisect each half. Cut along the diagonal lines. When you pick up the pieces, you will be holding four skinny, pointed giraffe legs.

of the head. This will give the giraffe head the proper tilt when it is attached to the neck and prevent your giraffe from obsessively studying the sky. *Do not remove the foam plug inside the circular cut, as it will fit inside the cardboard tube to give the head-neck attachment greater security.*

5. Now it's time to attach the two head knobs, those two protuberances which look a little like carpeted horns and are characteristic of most self-respecting giraffes. Place the ends of the two small cardboard tubes against the top of the giraffe head in the area between the ears. Use the orange felt-tip marker to draw a circle around each

tube. With these markings as your guides, carefully make two circular cuts about 1" deep into the giraffe head with the utility knife. *Do not remove the foam plugs, which form the inside of the circular cuts.* Spread a thin layer of white glue along the bottom inch of a small tube, inside and out. Push the glue-covered end of the tube firmly into one of the circular cuts on the top of the giraffe head. The inside of the foam circle should now be inside the tube. Repeat this procedure with the other small tube. Allow the glue to dry for at least one hour.

6. Spread a thin layer of white glue along the bottom inch inside and out-

FIRST SESSION

Materials

- two drop cloths or several newspapers
- prepared giraffe body
- prepared head-and-neck assembly
- tempera paint mixture (1 part white to 2 parts orange)
- individual paint containers (one per child)
- paintbrushes
- four pointed giraffe legs
- yardstick
- brown twine or yarn
- scissors

Preparing the Work Area

1. Cover an area of floor with one of the drop cloths or lots of newspaper. Unfold the giraffe body and spread it out flat on the drop cloth, so that the entire top side can be painted. If you used white poster board for the legs, lay them out for painting as well. The undersides of the giraffe body and legs do not need to be painted. Drape a chair with newspapers or a drop cloth, then prop the head-neck arrangement over the back of it so that children can easily approach it for painting. The entire head and neck will need a coat of paint.

2. Put out a sufficient supply of the orange-white tempera paint; make sure the paint is not too runny. An individual container for each child is best—one that can be held comfortably in one hand. Small plastic yogurt containers work well. Each child will also need a paintbrush.

3. Set aside the other materials until needed.

Completing the First Part of the Project

1. Children can now paint the giraffe body, head and neck. If the legs are made from white poster board, they should be painted orange also. Allow paint to dry overnight.

2. After the painting is completed, the children can work on the tail. Use a yardstick to measure off an 18" piece of twine or yarn. Have a student cut about thirty of these and line them up side-by-side. Save leftover material for a giraffe mane. Help children connect the strands together by tying a knot in the top of the bunch. They can then braid the tail or tie the strands together with smaller pieces of yarn. The last 3" or 4" of tail should be allowed to bush out.

SECOND SESSION

Materials

- construction paper—twelve sheets of brown or black as well as an assortment of colors
- white household glue
- children's scissors
- leftover twine or yarn
- painted giraffe body
- painted head-and-neck assembly
- four orange giraffe legs
- medium-size nail or Phillips screwdriver with a narrow shaft
- stapler (pliers-type, if you have it)
- 1 1/2" x 12" strip of heavy-duty cardboard or piece of cloth strapping
- four paper fasteners
- prepared tail

Preparing the Work Area

1. Set out the construction paper, glue, scissors and leftover yarn or twine next to the painted giraffe parts. Spread out the giraffe legs near the cardboard body.

2. Make sure that the nail, or screwdriver, stapler, strapping, paper fasteners and tail are nearaby for later use.

Completing the Project

1. Have children cut the twine or yarn into short pieces. They can glue these pieces along the top of the giraffe neck to create a mane. A few strands added to the tops of the giraffe head knobs look very stylish.

2. While students are working on the mane, place two giraffe legs on each curved side of the body. The wider top of each leg should overlap the outside of the body by 2". Push the point of the nail or screwdriver through both leg and body in the center of the area where they overlap. Poke a paper fastener through this hole and spread its flanges open inside the body. Make sure the leg swings easily back and forth. If not, loosen the paper fastener a little. Repeat this procedure with the other legs.

3. Direct children to cut facial features for their giraffe (eyes, mouth, eyelashes) from construction paper and glue them to the head. Spots and blotches can be cut from the brown or black construction paper and glued to the body, legs and neck. Encourage children to use only small amounts of glue so it will dry quickly and drip less. Cut hooves from the construction paper and glue them to the bottoms of the legs. Allow the glue to dry.

4. Ask two puppeteers to stand one behind the other. Lift up the giraffe body and place it on top of them with the sides and legs hanging down. Staple a piece of strapping across the front of the giraffe body, about 3" down from the center fold line. Attach the ends of the strapping firmly to the inside of the

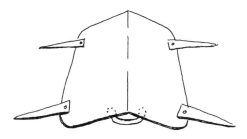

Attach the legs and neck strapping to the giraffe body.

cardboard body. Place two or three staples at each end. This strapping will help support the weight of the giraffe neck tube. Starting just above the strapping, slide the lower end of the neck tube into the giraffe body until the child in the front part of the giraffe has a firm grasp on it. Make sure the head is right-side up.

5. Staple the tail to the back end of the giraffe. Voila! You are standing next to one terrific giraffe.

Animating the Puppet

Give children time to practice moving together. They will be in character if they move slowly and with dignity. Children can practice nodding and shaking the head, searching for predators and stretching the neck in search of tasty leaves in imaginary treetops.

Variations

• If you cannot lay your hands on a hunk of foam rubber for the giraffe head, construct a lumpy but lovable head from a brown paper grocery bag.

Fill it halfway with loosely wadded newspaper. Push one end of the neck tube all the way into the bag. You want the tube to be surrounded by newspaper but close to one of the bag's narrow side panels. Most of the stuffed head will hang down to one side. Close the empty half of the bag around the tube and tape firmly in place with masking tape. Attach head knobs and ears with masking tape. Follow the same directions for painting and decorating this giraffe head as for the foam head.

Shortcut

• Create a simple two-dimensional puppet operated by one person for a quick cameo appearance. This puppet is the most recognizable part of the giraffe! Draw the side profile of a giraffe head and its long neck on a large piece of sturdy cardboard. Cut it out and let children paint and decorate it. When finished, the giraffe can poke its head above the curtain or from its side. The head might appear first, then more and more neck could come into view.

Saw-Toothed Lion

This puppet treats its makers to the finger-dabbling pleasures of papier-mâché. Think of it—a two-person puppet offering all the messy, skin-tingling fun of mud pies plus an end product with a great deal more eye appeal. How can you resist?

This is not a puppet which can be whipped out in an hour or two. You will need to allow several days for its completion. Don't let this deter you; most of the time required for its construction is drying time. Once you have prepared the foundation work on this puppet ("Paving the Way"), allow students two work sessions to complete it. In the first session, children will sculpt the lion's facial features with papier-mâché. It is a good idea for children to work in a room with a convenient sink, so they can easily wash the papier-mâché paste off their hands. After the papier-mâché has dried, students can complete the decoration and development of their lion puppet in a second session. Allow at least one hour for each of the children's work sessions, and allow a minimum of two to five days for the papier-mâché to dry. If this creates a scheduling problem, check out the shortcut suggestion at the end of the following instructions.

Preparation Materials

- **sturdy cardboard box 9" to 11" wide x 16" to 24" long x 10" to 14" deep**
- **cutting board or old piece of carpet**
- **steak or utility knife**
- **ruler**
- **pencil**
- **medium-size nail or Phillips screwdriver with a narrow shaft**
- **two paper fasteners, each at least 1" long**
- **strip of sturdy cardboard or cloth strapping about 15" x 2"**
- **stapler (pliers-type works best)**

Construction Prep

1. Place the cardboard box on its bottom on top of the cutting board or section of old carpet. Using a steak or utility knife, cut off the top flaps of the box so that only the sides and bottom remain. The bottom of the box will become the top of the lion's head. Cut a shoulder slot into one of the long sides of the box, leaving about 8" of solid, uncut box from the bottom of the box to the curved end of the shoulder slot, 3" from the back of the box to the back straight edge of the shoulder slot, and 5" between the front and back straight edges of the shoulder slot. The shoulder slot will be 5" wide, but its height will depend on the depth of the box you are working with. Cut a matching shoulder slot directly across from the first on the other long side of the box.

2. Every lion worth his mane needs an impressive set of teeth. Draw a line of bold and daring zigzags 3" to 4" deep across the inside of the front end and sides of the box. The upper point of each zigzag should be at least 2" below the top edge of the box. Zigzags should extend around both sides of the box to about 1/3 of the box's length, leaving at least 3" of untouched box between the zigzags and each shoulder slot. Extend the last tooth line on each side so that it runs straight up to the open top of the box.

3. This step is a little tricky, so take your time. You will need to remove the

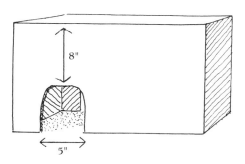

Cut one shoulder slot in the long side of the cardboard box, and cut a matching slot directly across from it.

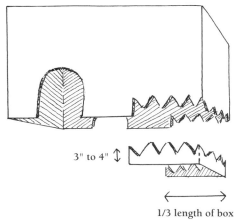

Draw a jagged line to represent large, carnivorous teeth. Cut carefully along this line to remove the lower jaw in one piece.

73

zigzag cutout in one piece. Lay the box on its side on top of the cutting board or old piece of carpet. Cut along the zigzag tooth line, rotating the box as you progress so that the part you are cutting rests on the board or carpet. Carefully remove and save the resulting jagged strip of cardboard, as this will become the lion's lower jaw.

4. Turn the box onto its bottom, and position the lower jaw so its jagged edges face the jagged edges on the box. Both end sections of the jaw should overlap the area of the box in front of the shoulder slots. Use the nail or screwdriver to poke a small hole through both layers in the center of the overlapping areas. Place a paper fas-

tener through each hole and secure it. You should now have a freely moving hinged jaw. Your lion will have a slight overbite, but who's going to point this out to a lion?

5. It's a good idea to attach a reinforcing piece of strapping to both sides of the box in the space between the jaw hinges and shoulder slots. The strapping should stretch across the width of the box and overlap each side of the box on the inside by approximately 2". Make sure this strapping will not interfere with the lion's jaw movement, then staple it securely into place. This strip will give a steadying handhold to the child wearing the lion's head.

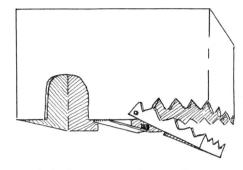

Attach the lower jaw with paper fasteners, and secure a piece of strapping between the arm holes and jaw hinge.

CHILDREN'S ACTIVITY

FIRST SESSION

Materials

- **drop cloth or large plastic trash bag**
- **prepared box for lion's head**
- **various size paper cups, small boxes, tubes, newspaper**
- **masking tape**
- **several brown grocery bags**
- **cellulose wallpaper paste powder, quart container of water, mixing bowl**
- **smocks**
- **pictures of lions' side profiles (optional)**

- **tan or light brown tempera paint, paintbrushes (optional)**

Preparing the Work Area

1. Place the drop cloth on a table and put the prepared lion's head on top. Set out the paper cups, boxes, tubes, newspaper and masking tape next to the head.

2. Set aside the brown paper bags, wallpaper paste, water, bowl and smocks in a convenient location.

3. Display illustrations or photographs of lions in a prominent place so children can easily refer to them.

Completing the First Part of the Project

1. Children can add shape to the box so it will more closely resemble a lion's head. Explain that they can use any of the small boxes, cups, etc. to give the large box lion-like features. Tell them that they will be adding a mane on another day, so they should focus on the shape of the lion's head during this session. What part bulges out? What part sticks up? It will be helpful if you can show them a few pictures of a lion's head so they can see the ins and outs of the lion's profile. Students should attach any objects they add firmly in place with masking tape. Newspaper can also be wadded up into desired shapes and taped into place.

2. Once children have completed this foundation work, they should tear the brown grocery bags into strips; do not cut paper with scissors, as ragged edges will blend more smoothly. The strips should be roughly 1" to 3" wide and 6" to 7" long. While students are tearing strips, mix the papier-mâché paste. Dump half of the quart of water (2 cups) into the bowl, and add about 2 tablespoons of cellulose wallpaper paste powder; mix together. Keep the rest of the water nearby in case the paste needs thinning.

3. Ask children to roll up their sleeves and put on smocks. Demonstrate papier-mâché technique by dipping one of the brown paper strips into the paste so that it is coated on both sides. Hold the strip by one end over the bowl, and lightly run your thumb and index finger down the length of the strip, wiping off excess paste. Drape the prepared strip over one of the taped-on features, and smooth it into place. The children should apply overlapping strips of papier-mâché until all of the taped on features and pieces of masking tape are covered. Strips should run in different directions and be smoothed down as they are applied. Any words or logos which were on the cardboard box can also be covered up with the papier-mâché strips. Make sure that none of the strips interfere with the opening and closing of the lion's mouth. When students have finished applying the strips, ask them to give their work one last

smoothing with their hands, making sure that all the strips lie flat against the surface. Once they have finished, children should clean their hands under running water—before they start sticking to the walls.

Allow the papier-mâché work sufficient time to dry. This should take two to five days, depending on the amount of papier-mâché paste used and the moisture level in the air. The lion will appear to be a little lumpy and drab at this point, but do not be discouraged. The noble beast will soon emerge.

4. If, when dry, the colors of the brown paper and the cardboard box differ too much, the lion's head may look splotchy. This can be remedied by giving the lion head a base coat of tan or light brown tempera paint. Allow to dry.

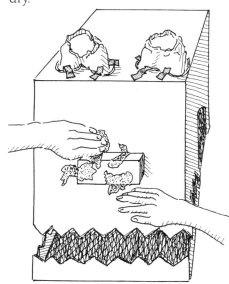

This lion has a cardboard box snout and ears made from flattened and curved paper cups. After children have added dimension to the lion head, they can cover the cardboard shapes and masking tape with strips of brown paper dipped in papier-mâché paste.

SECOND SESSION

Materials

- **construction paper in assorted colors (Make sure there is plenty of black and brown.)**
- **pencils**
- **white household glue**
- **clear plastic tape**
- **children's scissors**
- **piece of lightweight cloth roughly 2 yards x 1 1/2 yards**
- **stapler (pliers-type works best)**
- **brown or black yarn**
- **pipe cleaners (optional)**
- **craft stick, large or small**
- **masking tape**

Preparing the Work Area

1. Place the construction paper, pencils, glue, tape and scissors next to the lion's head.

2. Store the cloth, stapler, yarn, pipe cleaners (optional), craft stick and masking tape nearby until needed.

Completing the Project

1. Have children cut the construction paper into strips roughly 12" x 1", and glue one end of each strip to the lion's head to form his mane. This mane will look more dynamic if a slight fold is made near one end of each strip and the small folded area is glued to the

75

lion's head. Use a small piece of clear plastic tape to secure this glued end in place, if needed.

If you prefer a curly mane, roll each strip of construction paper tightly around a pencil before attaching it to the lion. Or accordion-fold each strip before attaching it, for a bouncy zigzag effect.

2. Children can cut facial features (eyes, nose, white triangles over the teeth, etc.) from construction paper, and glue these to the lion's head. Attach whiskers, made from pipe cleaners or strips of construction paper, to sides of the lion's nose with clear plastic tape.

3. While the glue dries, construct the lion's tail. Children should cut twenty or thirty strands of yarn, each about 15" long. Line up these strands side-by-side. Tie the strands together with short pieces of yarn at several places along the length of the tail. You may have to provide some help with the knots. The last 4" of tail should remain untied so that it can bush out into a tufted tail tip.

4. The assisting adult should staple the craft stick to the inside center of the lion's lower jaw, with about 3" of its length protruding below the jaw. Reinforce with masking tape if needed. This stick will be the control rod, used to open and close the mouth.

5. Once the glue on the mane and features is dry, it's time to put the lion together and see just what kind of a feline you've got there. Spread the body cloth out on the floor. Center the

lion's head along one of the 1 1/2-yard edges of the cloth. Staple the cloth firmly to the back of the lion's head, placing staples in several places along the back edge of the box.

6. Ask the two children who will operate the puppet to try on the lion so you can decide where to put the tail. Puppeteers should stand one behind the other. The child in front should wear the head, grasping the strapping with one hand and the control rod with the other. The child standing behind should bend forward at the waist, placing both hands on the hips of the child in the lead. Drape the body cloth over the second child and lift a pinch of material near the back of the lion. Staple the top of the tail in place onto the material, being careful not to staple the cloth to the child underneath.

Animating the Puppet

Now the children get their chance to make their creation come alive. Have puppeteers practice moving forward together. The lead child can open and close the lion's mouth by moving the control rod up and down. The puppeteer in the rear can provide the lion's mighty roars. Encourage students to try a silent creep, a trot, a scanning of the surroundings, a yawn. If the lion is to have a speaking part in a story or play, give the children time to develop a voice that fits their idea of the character.

Variations

• Have children cut triangular claws out of poster board and glue them onto the toes of adult-size old socks for a set of homemade lion's paws. These lion-feet socks can be worn over their shoes.

• If you don't mind allowing for additional drying time, have children paint the lion's features with tempera paints after the papier-mâché has dried. Attach the mane and whiskers after the paint dries.

If you have a collection of mismatched socks, children can turn them into clawed lion's feet to be worn right over the puppeteers' shoes.

Shortcut

• If time is pressing, put the lion together more quickly by having the children make a poster board mask and draping themselves with a cloth body (See *Poster Board Animal Mask*, page 96).

Overbearing Ogre

Not only is this puppet bigger than a bread box, it looks as if it could eat a bread box for an appetizer. Three children work together to operate this gawky, glorious rod puppet. Its appearance in any show is guaranteed to send ripples of excitement through the audience; its majestic passage down a parade route will be greeted by fascinated gazes and appreciative murmurs. There is a major role for this puppet in a Japanese folktale described later in this book (See *The Ogre's Staircase* in Chapter 9).

PAVING THE WAY

Preparation Materials

- piece of sturdy, lightweight cloth approximately 8' x 9' (a king-size flat bed sheet works well)
- measuring tape
- piece of chalk
- sharp scissors
- stapler (pliers-type is best) or needle and thread
- four large brown paper grocery bags
- 4' long broomstick or other sturdy, smooth pole
- 32"-long sturdy, lightweight control rod
- duct tape or strong twine

Construction Prep

1. Spread the large piece of cloth on the floor, and fold it in half lengthwise. Use the chalk to draw an outline of the ogre's tunic on the cloth. Cut out the tunic, cutting through both layers of cloth at once. *Do not cut the fold line.* Sew or staple the edges of the two

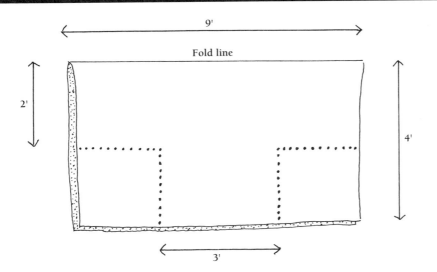

9'

Fold line

2'

4'

3'

Fold the cloth lengthwise and mark the tunic outline in chalk. Cut through both layers and sew matching sections together where indicated by the dotted lines.

pieces of cloth together, leaving the bottom and ends of the sleeves open. (If you cannot find a piece of cloth which is large enough, sew or staple smaller pieces together. Just make sure you leave the ends of the sleeve tubes and the bottom of the body tube open.) You should end up with a simple, serviceable garment for your typical unstylish ogre.

2. Open two of the large paper grocery bags. Put one inside the other to make a bag of double thickness, which will become the ogre's head.

3. Cut the remaining two grocery bags into four flat sheets of brown paper, which will be used later to make the ogre's hands. Simply cut free and discard the bottom of each bag, then cut along the entire length of one of the corner fold lines on each. Cut each of these long, flat sheets into two pieces of equal length. You now have four sheets of brown paper.

4. Lay the 4' broomstick or other sturdy pole on the floor to become the body control rod. Place the 32" control rod across the body control rod to form the shoulder crosspiece; position it 5" down from one end of the body rod and perpendicular to it, forming a cross. Securely fasten these two poles together in the area where they cross, using duct tape or strong twine. You don't want them slipping or sliding out of position once the ogre is in action.

CHILDREN'S ACTIVITY

Materials

- prepared double grocery bag
- pile of newspapers
- masking tape
- cardboard tube 15 1/2" long and wide enough to slide over the body

control rod (The cardboard tube from a roll of wrapping paper can be cut to the correct length.)

- drop cloth
- tempera paints in assorted colors
- paintbrushes
- electric blow drier (optional)

- white household glue
- crepe paper streamers, yarn or strips cut from plastic garbage bags
- cotton balls (optional)
- four sheets of brown paper from grocery bags
- construction paper in assorted colors

- two pairs children's scissors
- two pencils
- stapler (pliers-type is best)
- two broomsticks or other sturdy, smooth control rods, each about 3 1/2' long
- prepared cloth tunic
- prepared T-shape body control rod
- duct tape
- empty backpack (child-size, if available)
- piece of chalk

Preparing the Work Area

1. Put the prepared double grocery bag on the floor, open-end up, next to a pile of newspapers. Place the masking tape and 15 1/2" cardboard neck tube near at hand. Place a chair on top of a drop cloth. Set out paints and brushes on one corner of this drop cloth. Place nearby the white glue, streamers and yarn or plastic-bag strips. This will be the work space for creating the ogre's head.

2. Set up a neighboring work space for the two children who will make the ogre's hands. They will need access to the pile of newspaper (or cotton balls), the four sheets of grocery-bag paper, construction paper, glue, scissors and pencils. Store the two hand-control rods nearby.

3. Keep the other materials stored nearby until needed.

Completing the Project

1. The child who will be operating the head control rod can stuff the ogre's head, filling the double grocery bag with *loosely* wadded single sheets of newspaper. When the bag is nearly full, wiggle the cardboard tube well down into the center. It will be surrounded by newspaper wads, and its end should stick up out of the bag. Squeeze the bag opening closed around the tube; you may have to toss out a few newspaper wads if the bag is too full. Use masking tape to fasten the bag opening securely closed around the tube.

Turn the whole works over so the bag is on top, and tape the tube to a chair back, making the ogre's head accessible for painting. When the child has finished painting the ogre's features and the paint is sufficiently dry (you may use an electric blow drier to hasten the drying time), glue on the crepe-paper streamers, yarn or strips cut from plastic garbage bags to create the ogre's hair.

2. While the ogre's head is being worked on, the two children who will operate the ogre's arms should be constructing the giant's meaty paws. Provide them with pencils, brown paper sheets and scissors. Each child can design a hand, drawing each of them on one of the pieces of brown paper. Encourage students to make a large, fat-fingered hand—as large as the paper will allow. If children prefer, the ogre's hands might be mitten-shape paws.

Cut out the hand shape with the scissors. Children will need to make a matching hand by tracing around the first hand on their second piece of paper and cutting it out. Each child should end up with a matching pair of paper hands.

Once children have completed the tracing and cutting, an adult can staple the matching edges of each hand together around the fingers and the upper (thumb) edge of the hands, leaving the bottom edges and wrist areas open. Have children stuff the ogre's hands with small wads of newspaper or cotton balls.

Wriggle a 3 1/2' control rod well into the bottom edge of each hand back near the wrist area. Staple the hand edges closed, making sure that the rod

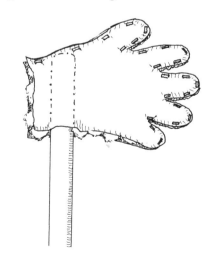

Insert a control rod parallel to the wrist opening in each hand. Then staple the open edges of hand together along the wrist and bottom.

end is secured firmly inside the hand. Use staples to stabilize the rod within the hand, and reinforce the bottom of the hand with masking tape in the area where the tube exits. The children can now cut pointed fingernails out of construction paper and glue them to the tips of the fingers.

3. When the paint and glue are dry, it's time to put your ogre together and see how it looks. Fit the ogre's tunic over the shoulder-body control rod. Cut a small hole in the middle of the top folded edge of the tunic so that the top 5" of the body rod (the neck rod) can poke through. Now lay the ogre's tunic on the floor, and stretch the sleeves out to their full length at each side. Place the hand-rods alongside the body at the end of the sleeves, one on each side with thumb-side up. Place the open end of each sleeve over the wrist of an ogre hand, and staple the end of each sleeve securely to both the stuffed hand and the hand control rod. Make sure that the end of each sleeve is firmly attached to its control rod.

Detach the ogre head-neck from the chair and slide the cardboard neck tube over the top part of the body control rod. After checking to make sure that the ogre is facing forward, secure the neck tube to the body rod with duct tape.

The puppeteer who will be carrying the head-body control rod should now put on the backpack, but should wear it in front of his or her chest. This will provide a convenient front pocket to

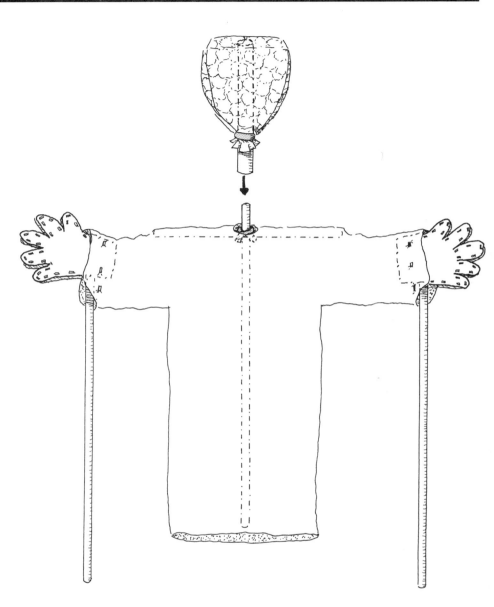

Assemble the ogre, making sure the ends of the sleeves are attached firmly to the hand control rods as there will be some tugging and pulling stress in this area when the puppet is in action.

help support the weight of the ogre's main control rod. The two hand puppeteers should get a firm grip on their control rods and—with an adult providing assistance at the ogre's shoulders—lift the big creature into standing position. Put the bottom end of the body rod into the backpack. Pull the bottom of the tunic over the head-body puppeteer's head, hiding the child's upper body inside the ogre's tunic. Use chalk to mark the area of tunic which covers the middle child's face. Lay the ogre down again and cut out the marked section to provide the child with a viewing window. Erect the ogre once again and give the children a chance to practice moving together.

Animating the Puppet

The ogre should move slowly and ponderously to befit its great bulk. Make sure that the children who are operating the ogre's hands look up to see what those hands are actually doing. The ogre's hands should be kept out and away from the body for greater effect and more expressive gestures—otherwise, the ogre resembles a wounded chicken. Give the ogre a few exercises to give the puppeteers some practice coordinating the ogre's movements. Can the ogre stomp? Turn around? Rock back and forth? Scratch its head? Wave its arms angrily? Shake its head negatively? Pat its hair? Show surprise? Droop its arms and hang its head? Fold its arms across its chest? Wave good-by? Take a bow?

Sit back and enjoy the show! This puppet is a fair amount of work, but the result is impressive. Give yourself a richly deserved pat on the back—or better yet, have the ogre give you one.

Variations

• If you have the time, enhance this puppet with a quick papier-mâché facial. Have children add shape to the ogre's head by dipping white paper towels or wads of white bathroom tissue into cellulose paste (2 tablespoons of cellulose wallpaper paste powder mixed into 2 cups of water). After they squeeze out excess paste, students can mold these moistened lumps into features on the ogre's bag head. When dry,

(two to five days) paint and decorate the head. This gives you an ogre with sculpted three-dimensional facial features—an ogre of craggy distinction!

• Use this three-rod puppet design to produce a fairy-tale giant or some other larger-than-life character to play a part in a parade or pageant. Mother Nature and Paul Bunyan are two of the limitless possibilities.

• Using the same basic three-rod design, scale the ogre down somewhat. A smaller ogre will be lighter and easier for younger children to manage.

• If the body cloth is somewhat gauzy and transparent, you will not have to cut a viewing window for the puppeteer inside.

Shortcuts

• If you'd like to speed up the process, cut the ogre's facial features out of construction paper or use brightly colored, lightweight objects which can be attached with glue or clear plastic tape. This will eliminate the paint-drying time.

• Construct the ogre's hands more quickly using a large pair of gloves. Stuff them with cotton balls. Twist one end of a hand control rod well into the wrist opening of each glove. Close the wrist opening around the control rod with duct tape. Wrap a sleeve end around the wrist area of each glove and its control rod, and secure with staples.

Sprightly Whirligig

This is a simplification of the Over-bearing Ogre puppet. One puppeteer can operate this puppet, twirling and dipping the whirligig about to create a dynamic presence. This dancing fool will liven up any parade or pageant. Imagine a snaking line of bobbing whirligigs gyrating to a lively tune provided by a marching kazoo band!

Preparation Materials

- three sturdy, rigid dinner-size paper plates
- scissors
- broomstick
- masking tape
- stapler (pliers-type is best)
- utility knife
- pencil
- cutting board

Construction Prep

1. Stack two of the plates, one inside the other. Cut a 1" slit through both plates, making the cut at any point along the edge of the plates and directing it in toward the center. Separate the plates. Lay one end of the broomstick over the inside surface of one of the plates. The end of the broomstick should stretch across most of the width of the plate and line up with the small slit. Tape the broomstick securely to the inside of the plate in this position. Place the second plate upside down on top of the pole and the taped plate, and line up the two plate edges and slits. Press the plates together gently; the slits should spread open slightly around the broomstick. Staple the plates together around the edges. Make sure you place a staple on each side of the broomstick where it exits the double plate arrangement. Reinforce the slit area of the two plates with masking tape. You have just completed the foundation for the puppet's head.

2. With the third plate right-side up, hold the free end of the control rod perpendicular against the center of the plate and trace around the end of the rod with a pencil, marking the circumference of the pole on the plate. Set the pole aside, place the plate on the cutting board and use the utility knife to cut an × inside the marked circle. *Do not remove any pieces of the plate.*

3. Push the free end of the control rod through the × incision on the paper plate. The × should open enough to allow you to press the rod through, although it will still grip the rod somewhat. Stop sliding the plate when it gets to a point just below the double-plate head at the top of the rod. Tape this collar plate firmly into position with masking tape, making sure it will not slide up or down the control rod.

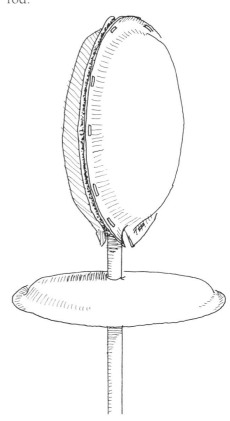

Tape the first plate parallel to one end of the broomstick. Line up the second plate with the first, plate bottoms facing out and broomstick between them. Staple their edges together. The third plate will provide an anchor for swirling streamers.

Materials

- prepared control rod-plate arrangement (one per puppet)
- masking tape
- construction paper in assorted colors
- children's scissors
- colorful lightweight objects such as small boxes, paper cups, foam pieces, sponges, plastic lids, pompoms
- white household glue and clear plastic tape
- lightweight streamers such as crepe paper streamers, strips of thin cloth, plastic surveyor's ribbon, strips cut from plastic garbage bags
- geometric stickers (optional)

Preparing the Work Area

1. Set the bottom of the control rod on the floor next to a chair or table leg and use masking tape to secure the rod in a standing position. The double-plate head and paper-plate collar should be readily accessible to the child who will be decorating it. Set out the construction paper, scissors and colorful lightweight objects nearby with the clear plastic tape and glue.

2. Set aside the streamers and stickers (if available) until needed.

Completing the Project

1. Have puppeteers construct the puppets' facial features and ears from the assorted lightweight objects and shapes cut from construction paper. Tape or glue these to the double-plate head.

2. Attach streamers to the edges of the paper plate collar with clear plastic tape or glue. Streamers can also be decorated with colorful geometric stickers for additional eye appeal. The streamers can be uniform or layered into different lengths. Shorter lengths will provide the whirligig with a springier head of hair.

Animating the Puppet

Once the glue has dried, release the puppet control rod from its bondage and pass it to the puppeteer. The child should hold the control rod firmly with both hands. The whirligig can be twirled, jiggled or swayed for lively effect. Give the puppet room to strut its stuff. This type of puppet really comes into its own when moving to music. Let the puppeteer decide what type of music or sound effects would be best.

If a child has trouble supporting this puppet, provide the puppeteer with a backpack—to be worn in front, over the chest. Put the bottom of the control rod into the backpack, which will support the weight so the puppeteer can use his or her hands to control the movement of the puppet.

Variations

- String bells onto pipe cleaners and wrap them around the control rod. The whirligig will provide its own festive sound effects.

- If additional drying time is not a problem, this puppet is a good candidate for papier-mâché work. Children can add shape to its head by dipping white paper towels or wads of white bathroom tissue into papier-mâché paste (two tablespoons of cellulose wallpaper paste powder mixed with two cups of water). After squeezing out excess paste, mold these moistened lumps into features on the paper-plate head. When dry, paint and decorate the head.

• You can easily develop the whirligig into a three-person rod puppet. You will need two additional control rods (broomsticks or yardsticks will do), duct tape, cotton balls, two 4' cloth ribbons and two large rubber or cloth gloves. While one child decorates the head, the other two can stuff the gloves with cotton balls. Insert the end of a control rod into the wrist opening of each glove. Tape each glove's wrist opening closed, and secure it to the rod with duct tape. Secure one end of a 4' length of ribbon to one of the control rods directly under the glove. Attach the free end of the ribbon to the head control rod just under the paper plate collar. Repeat this process with the other glove and ribbon. Now all three children can help attach streamers to the puppet's paper plate collar. Streamers may also be added to the two arm ribbons. Each child supports a control rod as the whirligig begins its lively promenade—with streamers jiggling and both hands fanning the air in a festive greeting.

If you wrap the gloved fingers of each of the puppet's hands around a pair of maracas and secure them with clear plastic tape or staples, the puppet can shake them about to create its own dancing rhythm.

FOUR

Simple Masks

....

Capturing Personality in Brown Paper Bag

The shy boy with oversize spectacles was quietly absorbed in the construction of his paper bag mask. When he placed it over his head, he became a gluttonous ogre—strutting across the room, rubbing his belly and motioning grandly for more food.

There is something magical about masks. Put on a mask, and your gestures are transformed into those of a clever princess, a spellbinding wizard, a craggy old grandmother. When children use masks to help tell a story, the audience will carry some of that magic home with them. Masks offer a wonderful opportunity to explore the value of gesture, the dynamics of body language and the wide range of human personality and interaction. The timid child can safely bellow and stomp, the boisterous child can experience the subtleties of slow and graceful movement. Masks provide children with a fascinating medium for polishing their powers of observation and communication.

Before children begin to work on masks, ask them to think about the variety of human characteristics and personalities they have encountered in books, on television or while people-watching in public places. Ask the children to consider the many possibilities: People can be young, old, energetic, cheerful, shy, awkward, comic, graceful, proud, timid, swaggering, sweet, pugnacious, greedy or mysterious. Encourage students to choose the human characteristics they would like their masks to convey before they begin working on them.

A mask-making project can stimulate reading and writing skills. Children might make a mask to portray a character from a book. They could produce written descriptions of fictional characters of their own invention, then make masks of those characters and use them to give brief demonstrations showing how their created characters would look, move and gesture. This could become a cooperative project if the children work as partners, with one child providing a sound effect accompaniment for a partner's masked character performance. Then they could trade places. Or you might give each child a chance to develop his or her own masked character, then assign them to small groups in which they could work together as a writing team—each group sitting down to develop a short plot involving the interaction of their characters. Groups could then give masked performances to act out their written descriptions.

Grocery Bag Mask

A large brown grocery bag provides an inexpensive foundation for a versatile wraparound mask. This mask enables its wearers to remain in character even when their backs are turned to the audience

Preparation Materials

- large brown paper grocery bag
- scissors
- ruler
- pencil

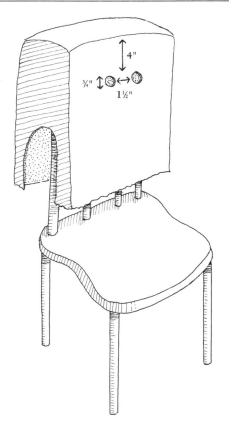

Cut peepholes into the bag in advance.

Construction Prep

1. Open up the grocery bag and set it on its bottom. Cut away the top half (nearest the bag's open end) of each narrow side panel. When the bag mask is worn over the head, these slots will provide room for the performer's shoulders.

2. Slide the bag, bottom-side up, over the back of a straight chair. Find its best broad side, and face that side toward you. (The best side would have few or no logos or other markings.) Measure 4" down from the bag's bottom and make a light pencil mark at this point near the center of the chosen side. Draw two 3/4" circles on either side of this pencil mark, spaced 1 1/2" apart at their inside edges. Cut these circles out, and your mask foundation now has peepholes.

CHILDREN'S ACTIVITY

Materials

- prepared grocery bag with peepholes (one per mask)
- assorted colors of oil pastels, crayons or tempera paints (If you choose to use paints, you will need paintbrushes and small, portable containers. You may also want to

protect the work area with newspapers or a drop cloth.)
- construction paper in various colors and lightweight decorations such as yarn, crepe paper streamers, curling ribbon, sequins, geometric stickers, feathers

- children's scissors
- white household glue
- clear plastic tape

Preparing the Work Area

1. If the children are going to use paints, drape the prepared grocery bags over the backs of straight-back chairs for easy access. Protect the chairs and floor with newspaper. Place the paints and brushes on a nearby table. (The paints can be poured into small, portable containers and the color of choice carried over to the mask while it is being used.)

2. If crayons or oil pastels are used, bags can be decorated on a worktable. Make sure the coloring agents are easily accessible.

3. Set up a separate table with decorating supplies, scissors, tape and glue.

Completing the Project

1. Before children begin to make their masks, demonstrate how the mask will be worn to orient students as to top, bottom, front and back. Point out the peepholes and let them know that these holes will let them see where they are going when they are the wearing masks. Emphasize that the faces on their masks need not be limited by these little peepholes. Their mask faces could have big owlish eyes or crinkly laughing eyes, which need not be located around the peepholes. The bags are much bigger than their own faces, so the features on their masks can also be larger. Before they begin to decorate their masks, have children try them on. If anyone has trouble seeing through their peepholes, use scissors to enlarge them.

2. Point out the location of the coloring agents and invite children to begin. Remind them that their masks have backs and sides which can also be decorated.

3. Once students have finished with the coloring agents, suggest that they take a look at the options on the decorations table. They may find materials they want to use to design hair, mustaches, eyebrows and earrings, or they may want to cut paper shapes to help them develop masks with distinct personality. Strips of construction paper can be accordion-folded or curled for dynamic hair. Paper ears and noses can be cut, folded and attached by an edge so they project out from the mask and add more dimension.

Using the Mask

This mask enables its wearer's hands to be free for gesturing and carrying props. The wraparound style makes it unnecessary for the wearer to constantly face the audience. Give children an opportunity to practice moving and gesturing while wearing their masks. Because of the relatively large size of this mask, it is ideal for children wishing to portray an ogre, giant, dancing bear or overbearing and vainglorious villain.

Variation

• When you are doing the foundation work on these masks, drape the bags over the backs of chairs and give the outside of each bag a base coat of white tempera paint mixed with a dollop of white glue. This will help cover up any logos and provide a lighter palette. When this base coat has dried and you are ready for children to begin working on the masks, the decorations will be brighter and the colors stronger.

Paper Plate Mask

This is an inexpensive yet expressive mask which can be made quickly and easily. Any shape of paper plate can provide the foundation. It is only required that the plate have an unadorned white paper bottom and be large enough to cover a child's face.

Preparation Materials

- **paper plate with plain white bottom (Lunch, dinner and platter sizes all work well.)**
- **pencil**
- **ruler**
- **small sharp scissors or utility knife**
- **poster board or thin cardboard**

Construction Prep

1. Place the plate, bottom up on a table. Draw two circles on the plate's bottom, locating them in the central area of the plate. Each circle should be about 3/4" across. For best visibility the circles should be 1 1/2" apart at their inside edges.

2. Cut out the circles with the scissors or utility knife. (Protect the surface of the table if you are using a utility knife.) Your mask now has a set of peepholes.

3. Draw a U-shape nose slot below the two peepholes. Locate the curved bottom of the U at a level is 1 1/2" below the bottom edge of the peepholes; the topmost points of the U should be 1" apart and at a level approximately 1/2" below the bottom of the peepholes.

4. Cut along the U-shape pencil line, but *do not remove any part off the resulting nose flap.*

5. Cut a strip 1" x 20" from the poster board.

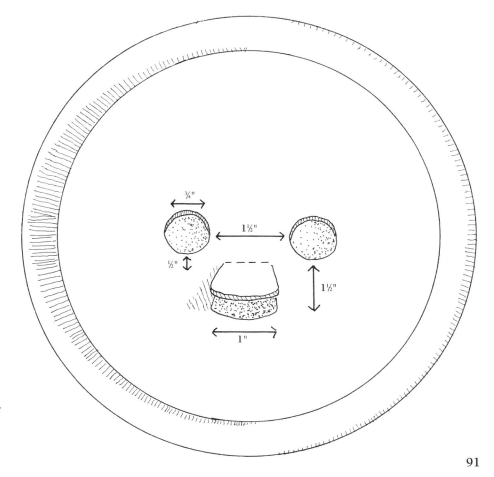

Cut a nose flap and peepholes into the paper plate.

CHILDREN'S ACTIVITY

Materials

- prepared plate (one per mask)
- felt-tip markers in assorted colors
- clear plastic tape
- white household glue
- construction and tissue paper in assorted colors
- children's scissors
- lightweight decorations such as crepe paper streamers, pom-poms, feathers, pipe cleaners, glitter glue, tree tinsel, curling ribbon, scraps of wrapping paper)
- poster board strip (at least one per mask)
- stapler
- adult scissors

Preparing the Work Area

1. Set up a table with a prepared plate, white bottom up, at each child's work space. Fan out the markers, tape, glue, construction paper, tissue paper and scissors along the center of the table within easy reach of all.

2. Spread out the lightweight decorations on a separate table.

3. Store the poster board strips, stapler and adult scissors nearby for later use.

Completing the Project

1. Hold one of the prepared plates in front of your face and look out through the peepholes to demonstrate how the mask will be worn. The plain white bottom of the plate is the part which should face out, and it is the surface of the mask which is to be decorated. Show students the nose slot. Point to the peepholes and explain that these will enable them to see where they are going when they wear their masks. Children should hold their plates up to their faces to test the peepholes. Enlarge the peepholes for any child who needs it.

Encourage students to decorate their masks in any way they like. The eyes might be much bigger than the peepholes, or they might be placed above, below or outside the peepholes. Point out the markers and colorful paper, which children can use to design their masks. Have students draw facial features directly onto the plate, cut them out of construction paper and glue them to the plate, or use a combination of these techniques. Construction paper ears might be attached to the edge of the plate. Paper features could be folded or curled to increase the visual interest and add dimension to their masks.

2. Once children have finished working with the materials at their table, invite them to look at the supplies on the decorations table and choose any

items they would like to add to their masks.

3. As children complete their masks, staple a poster board support band to each mask. Attach one end of the poster board strip to the outside edge of the plate at a spot level with the peepholes. The child should then hold the mask in position as you stretch the poster board strip around the back of the child's head and over to the opposite edge of the plate, again at peephole level. Make it a fairly snug fit. You will probably have some leftover poster board hanging down. Hold the poster board firmly against the plate's edge where the two meet. Remove the mask from the child's head. Staple the cardboard strip to the plate at this point. Cut off any excess strip length with a pair of scissors.

Using the Mask

This mask is lightweight and comfortable (thanks to the nose flap). The poster board headband leaves children's hands free to gesture. Body movement is unimpeded. Give children an opportunity to practice moving in a style which they feel fits the personality of their masks. A large mirror makes a great teaching aid at this point. If a mirror is unavailable, children may want to choose a partner. They can then take turns observing each other's movements, offering feedback and suggestions.

Because these masks are two-dimensional, you may have to remind children to face the audience when wearing them.

Variations

• If children have trouble keeping their masks in position, increase the stability by adding an additional strip of poster board. Attach one end of the strip to the center of the top edge of the mask, and loop it over the top of the child's head and down to the original headband at the center back of the child's head. Staple the straps together where they meet. You now have a headband with horizontal and vertical support—like a baseball catcher's mask. Paper or cloth strips can be glued or stapled to this extra strap to provide the mask with a lively head of hair. Add more strips if additional foundation is required for hair or head ornaments.

A few simple changes produce interesting variations of the basic Paper Plate Mask.

If the completed mask slides around on the child's head, attach an additional poster board strap extending across the top and down the back of the head.

• Staple a piece of lightweight cloth or a sheet of tissue paper to the top of the mask and drape it over the child's head. This will cover the child's hair and increase the mystery of the mask. The bottom edge of the cloth or tissue paper can be cut into strips to simulate the hair of the masked persona.

• Eliminate the poster board headbands, and staple a craft stick control rod to the bottom of the plate. Because children can now hold their masks a few inches out from their faces, it will no longer be necessary to cut nose flaps into the plates. However, holding the masks now occupies one of their hands, limiting them to one-handed gestures.

• Using the control rod approach, staple two plates together, plate bottoms facing out, with a control rod protruding from their shared bottom edge.

Each side of the mask can be developed into a different character or facial expression. Have the student choose which side to present to the audience. A simple flip of the plate enables one child to play two roles or express two conflicting emotions. Don't bother cutting peepholes for this type of mask. Children will be able to see where they are going if they hold their masks a few inches out in front of their faces.

• The paper plate mask can easily be adapted into a speaking mask by cutting away the portion of the plate which covers the child's nose and mouth. (Do not remove the portion of the plate which covers the cheeks.) The child's own mouth and nose now function as those of the masked character.

Wind Mask

This is a another variation of the paper plate mask, but this version has special effects. This mask has a built-in handle through which the performer supplies wind power. It may be used to dramatize *Why Fish Can't Sing* (See Chapter 9).

PAVING THE WAY

Preparation Materials

- **paper plate with plain white bottom (a sturdy, rigid plate works best)**
- **ruler**
- **pencil**
- **scissors**
- **utility knife and cutting board (optional)**
- **cardboard tube 4" or 5" long x 1" to 2" across (Use a cardboard bathroom tissue tube or half of a paper towel tube, or make a tube from a rolled-up index card.)**
- **tissue paper in various colors**
- **shoebox or other container**

Construction Prep

1. Lay the plate bottom up on a flat surface. Draw a 3" x 1" rectangle in the middle of the plate bottom. Cut the rectangle out with the scissors, or use a utility knife and cutting board. This opening will provide the performer with a viewing window.

2. Place one end of the cardboard tube perpendicular against the plate, 1" below the bottom edge of the eye slit and centered along its length. With a pencil, trace around the end of the tube. Remove the tube and cut out this circle. This will be the blow hole; the end of the tube should fit snugly into it.

3. Cut the tissue paper into strips roughly 4" x 1/2". Put the strips into the shoebox.

Materials

- prepared paper plate (one per mask)
- cardboard tube (one per mask)
- felt-tip markers in various colors
- white household glue
- clear plastic tape
- shoebox with tissue paper strips

Preparing the Work Area

1. Place a prepared plate, bottom up, and a tube at each child's work place. Make felt-tip markers accessible to all.

2. Store the glue, tape and box of paper strips nearby for later use.

Completing the Project

1. Let children know that they will be making wind masks. They can decorate their tubes and plate bottoms with markers in whatever designs and colors they feel best represent their impressions of the wind.

2. Once their decorations are complete, help students attach their tubes to their plates. Insert the very end of each tube into the matching hole in the plate bottom; the rest of the tube should project out from the plate's bottom surface, which will be the front of the mask. Use several strips of tape to secure the end of the tube to the plate. Tape the tube to the inside of the mask (the eating surface of the plate) so the tape won't show.

3. Place the paper strips and glue on the table. Show children how to attach the strips to the inside edge of the projecting end of the tube. They only need to apply a small dot of glue to one end of each paper strip before sticking it onto the tube. The small amount of glue used should dry in a very short time.

Using the Mask

Have children position their masks in front of their faces by holding onto the cardboard tubes and looking through the eye slits. When the children blow through their tubes, the brightly colored strips of paper will dance in the breeze.

Challenge the children to invent a good moaning or wailing wind sound which they can produce at the same time they are blowing the tissue strips about. This is trickier than it sounds—try it.

Poster Board Animal Mask

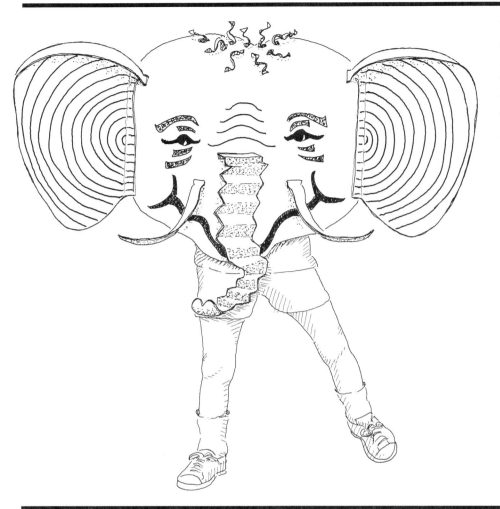

This mask is large, lightweight and easy to make. If your story requires the appearance of a large animal and your preparation time is limited, this is the mask for you. However, the performer will use both hands to hold this mask, so don't plan on any hand gestures.

PAVING THE WAY

Except for gathering a few materials together, there is little preparation needed for this mask. It would be helpful to the children if you could find pictures or photos showing a front view of the facial features of the animals involved.

Materials

- 22" x 28" sheet of white poster board (one per mask)
- pencils
- crayons or oil pastels in assorted colors
- construction paper in assorted colors
- white household glue
- clear plastic tape
- children's scissors (one pair per child)
- pipe cleaners (two per mask)
- duct tape
- pictures showing front view of animals (optional)

Preparing the Work Area

1. Set up a worktable or clear a work area on the floor. Place a sheet of poster board and a pencil at each child's work space. Place the crayons and oil pastels where they can be easily reached by all mask makers.

2. Place the construction paper, glue, tape and scissors on a nearby desk or table. Set aside the pipe cleaners and duct tape until needed.

3. If available, display animal pictures prominently.

Completing the Project

1. Before children start to work on their masks, encourage them to think big. They should make their animal faces as large as the poster board will allow, going right to the edges as much as possible. Instruct children to draw a front view of the animal's face—as if the animal were staring right at them. Let students know that construction paper will be available if they wish to add ears, manes, tongues or trunks to the animal's basic head shape. They may plan their mask with a pencil or start right in with colors. After coloring their animal heads, have them cut off any surplus poster board.

2. Add construction paper ears, manes, tongues and other distinguishing characteristics to the masks. Glue or tape one edge of each addition to the poster boards. The visual interest of the mask is increased if ears and manes are extended out from the edge of the mask, where they will be animated by air currents and mask movement.

3. After masks are complete, flip them over and secure pipe cleaner handles to the backside with duct tape. (See "Completing the Project" step two of the *Adaptable Multi Puppet* in Chapter 2.)

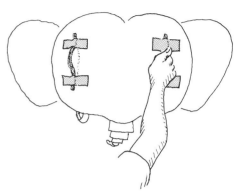

Attach arched pipe cleaner handles to the back of the mask with duct tape.

Using the Mask

The child using this mask should attempt to face the audience as much as possible. Hand gestures are not possible but the masked performer can vary body movements—jumping, prancing, stomping, stalking and trembling. The head can nod its agreement or move from side to side in refusal. Give performers time to experiment with different types of body motion, walking styles and leg positions.

Variations

• Use a piece of cloth 2 yards x 1 1/2 yards to transform a poster board animal mask into a two-person puppet. Drape the cloth over two children, standing one behind the other and bending forward at the waist. The child in front holds the mask. A tail can be constructed out of paper or yarn and safety pinned to the back end of the cloth.

• This type of mask need not be limited to animal characters. It could easily provide the facial characteristics for an oafish ogre, a bashful troll or a shimmering, beribboned sun sliding gracefully across the room.

Papier-Mâché Mask

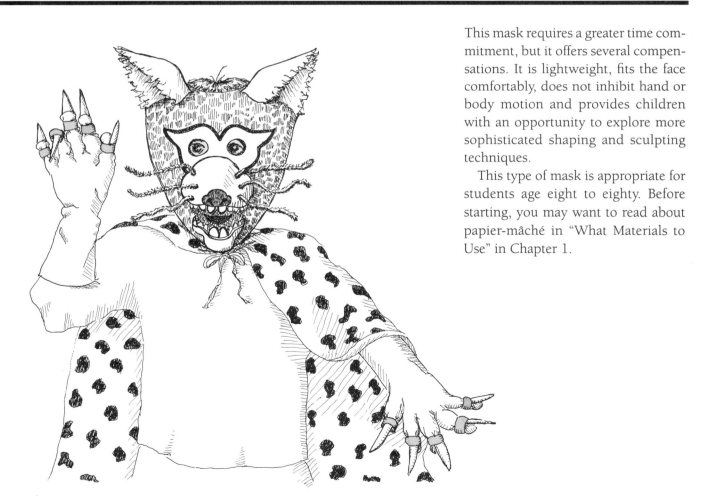

This mask requires a greater time commitment, but it offers several compensations. It is lightweight, fits the face comfortably, does not inhibit hand or body motion and provides children with an opportunity to explore more sophisticated shaping and sculpting techniques.

This type of mask is appropriate for students age eight to eighty. Before starting, you may want to read about papier-mâché in "What Materials to Use" in Chapter 1.

The adult preparation time for this mask spans several days, as the mask is constructed in layers and each layer requires drying time. Set up in an area where you will be able to leave your work in progress for a week or so. Applying layers of papier-mâché is hand-pleasing work requiring no great powers of concentration. You can listen to your favorite music or converse with a friend while you work.

If you want to make more than one mask foundation, build on several masks molds at once, assembly-line fashion, or allow plenty of time and use one goalie-mask mold repeatedly until you complete the desired number of foundations.

One word of warning: Papier-mâché is an enjoyably messy hands-on activity, but you will need to clean your hands under running water. If possible set up your work area near a sink, because the minute you plunge your hands into the paste—the phone will ring.

When planning for the children's participation, allow time for three separate sessions. If your schedule cannot accommodate this time commitment, skip ahead to the "Shortcuts" recommended at the end of these instructions.

PAVING THE WAY

Preparation Materials

- plastic drop cloth or garbage bag
- clear plastic wrap
- hockey goalie mask with straps removed (You can find these masks in sports stores, and they are sometimes sold as Halloween masks in discount stores. An inexpensive plastic model is fine.)
- large brown paper grocery bag
- cellulose wallpaper paste powder
- water
- bowl for mixing paste
- aluminum foil
- thin felt-tip marker or pencil
- utility knife and cutting board or mat of old carpet, or sturdy scissors
- several sheets of white newsprint

Construction Prep

1. Spread the plastic drop cloth or garbage bag over your work space. Mold a sheet of plastic wrap loosely over the outer surface of the goalie mask and tuck the excess plastic wrap underneath it. This plastic coating will keep the papier-mâché from adhering to the goalie mask mold. Set the wrapped mold faceup on the drop cloth.

2. Tear, do not cut, the brown paper bag into several strips roughly 2" x 10".

3. Roll up your sleeves and make the papier-mâché paste by mixing the cellulose powder with water: two cups water to two tablespoons powder. Add more water if the paste gets too thick. You may have to make additional paste if you use it up before mask preparations are complete.

4. Dip a strip of brown paper into the paste and run it between your thumb and fingers until both sides of the paper have a thin coating of paste and any excess paste is scraped off. Or dip your hands into the paste and rub the strip between your hands until it is thinly coated. Lay the prepared strip across the plastic-covered goalie mask. Smooth it down so that it molds itself to the shape of the hockey mask. Repeat this process with another strip. Add more strips until the facial surface of the goalie mask is completely covered, eyeholes and all. The strips should run in different directions and overlap each other for strength. Don't worry if some of the strips extend beyond the edges of the mask and onto the plastic garbage bag. Make sure you smooth down each strip to make complete contact with the mask, eliminating air pockets and pressing edges down. Continue adding strips until the mask is covered with overlapping strips two or three layers thick. The brown paper is a little stiff to work with but it will give your mask a strong foundation.

5. Cover the bowl with foil to preserve any leftover paste. Wash your hands. Allow the papier-mâché to dry, which can take two to five days depending on conditions. The papier-mâché will dry in a shorter time if the air is dry and the room has good ventilation. It will dry even more quickly outdoors on a sunny warm day. A session with a portable hair drier will also speed up the drying process.

Once the papier-mâché mask is dry on the outside, lift it off the hockey mask. You may have to wiggle and rock it slightly to pop it off. Flip the mask upside down and allow its underside to dry.

6. Once this paper foundation is dry, remove the plastic wrap from the goalie mask. Place the papier-mâché mask facedown on your work surface. Put the hockey mask facedown inside it. Using the goalie mask eyeholes as your guide, mark the positions for two eyeholes on the inside of your papier-mâché mask. The holes should be about 1" across and 1 1/2" apart at their inside edges. Mark a small horizontal slit about 1" x 1/2" in the middle of the mouth area. Remove the papier-mâché mask and set it facedown on a cutting board or the mat from an old carpet. Use a utility knife or sturdy scissors to cut out the eyes

and mouth. Then place the goalie mask inside the papier-mâché mask, and use your scissors to remove any excess brown paper which may extend beyond the goalie mask. Restore the plastic wrap to its former position over the surface of the goalie mask.

7. Tear the newsprint into strips of three sizes, making a separate pile for each size strip. One pile should consist of strips about 1" x 6", another pile of strips approximately 1" x 2", and a third pile of strips about 1" x 1/2'.

8. Place the brown paper mask (minus its goalie mask mold) on the drop cloth. Uncover the paste. Start your work with the smallest strips. Dip the strip into the paste, remove the excess paste and poke one end if it into the mouth slit of the papier-mâché mask. Smooth one end down against the inside surface of the mask, wrap the strip over a section of the rough-cut edge of the mouth slit, and smooth the other end down against the outside surface of the mask. Continue applying and overlapping strips in this fashion until the entire rough-cut edge of the mouth slit is covered with white papier-mâché. Each eyehole should receive this treatment. Make sure each strip of paper is smoothed down completely on both inside and outside surfaces of the mask.

9. Now dip a medium-size strip into the paste, remove excess paste and apply it to the outside edge of the mask, bending it over the rough edge so it covers a section of this edge and

is smoothed down against the outer and inner surface of the mask. Continue this process until the entire outside edge of the mask is covered with white papier-mâché.

10. Return the papier-mâché mask to its former position on the plastic-covered goalie mask. Using the largest strips, cover the remaining brown surface areas of the mask with overlapping strips of white papier-mâché. Make sure the strips do not cover the eyeholes or mouth slit. If you end up with too much paper, just tear off the excess. When you are finished, you should not be able to see the underlying layers of brown paper on the surface of the mask. Smooth the strips down carefully to achieve a uniform surface. You may have to use smaller pieces of paper when working around the tip of the nose or covering other curved spots. Let the mask dry. When the surface seems dry, remove the mask from the goalie mold. Turn it over and let the inside surface dry.

CHILDREN'S ACTIVITY

FIRST SESSION

Materials

- plastic drop cloth or garbage bags
- prepared papier-mâché mask foundation (one per mask)
- work smock (one per child)
- cellulose powder
- water
- one or more mixing bowls
- aluminum foil
- plain white bathroom tissue
- plain white paper towels
- white newsprint
- small boxes, cardboard tubes, egg cartons, poster board, pipe cleaners
- scissors
- masking tape
- pictures or photos of a variety of masks (optional)
- goalie mask

Preparing the Work Area

1. This project works best if the children work standing at a table. Protect the table surface with plastic garbage bags or a large plastic drop sheet. This project involves drying time; if you are not able to leave masks out on the table for several days, you may want to set out individual work boards or trays which can be moved to a convenient drying area.

2. Place a paper-mâché mask foundation and smock at each child's work space. Mix up the cellulose paste, cover it with aluminum foil and set it on the table where it can be easily reached; you will need more than one paste container if you are working with a large group.

3. Scatter bathroom tissue, paper towels and newsprint around the center of the table where all have access to them.

4. Set out small cardboard boxes and tubes, egg cartons, poster board, pipe cleaners, scissors and masking tape for ready use at a neighboring table.

5. Display pictures of masks, if available, in a prominent spot.

6. Place the plastic goalie mask within easy reach.

Completing the First Part of the Project

1. Once children are in smocks with sleeves rolled up, let them know that they will be sculpting with papier-mâché. Encourage them to think about the mask they would like to make. Discuss the wide variety of options: bulbous nose, big ears, high cheekbones, curling horns, pouting mouth, crinkly eyes, etc. This would be a good time to point out the pictures of different masks, if you have them, and to talk

briefly about the various ways masks are used in other countries.

2. Talk about the papier-mâché process and use the goalie mask to demonstrate the techniques. Attach one of the cardboard tubes securely to the goalie mask with masking tape. The tube could be flattened, shaped with scissors and taped into position as an animal ear or pointed horn. Explain that this would be the first step toward adding a large or extending shape to a mask. Point out the tubes, poster board and other materials on the neighboring table.

3. Tear off a few strips of newsprint. Dip one into the paste. Spread paste onto both sides of the paper and remove the excess. Place the strip on the goalie mask so it will cover part of the cardboard tube and help to anchor it where it attaches to the mask. Show students how to smooth a strip down with their fingers. Explain that any items they add to their masks should be covered with strips of white newsprint papier-mâché for greater strength and a lighter painting surface.

4. Dip a wad of bathroom tissue into the paste, squeeze out the excess paste, and mold it into a desired shape such as a large, lumpy nose or a set of expressive lips. Let students know that they can use this technique with paper towels also. Leave the paper towels and bathroom tissue shapes uncovered if a rough-textured surface is desired, or covered with paste-dipped newsprint if a smooth finish is preferred.

5. Encourage children to think about faces as structures composed of different shapes, which can be exaggerated for greater effect. Students can make the eyes on their masks bigger than the cutout eyeholes if they wish, but they should remember not to cover these peepholes or the ventilating mouth slit with papier-mâché. Suggest that they concentrate on adding shape to their masks and not worry about colors, as they will be painting their masks on another day.

You may have to remind students to remove excess paste before applying papier-mâché to their masks. Explain that masks will take a very long time to dry if too much paste is used. Make sure children remember to smooth the edges down and press out any air bubbles. If they have trouble obtaining a smooth finish, they may need to use smaller paper strips.

6. Once students are finished, they can help put materials away, clean up any spills and wash their hands. While they are cleaning up, remove the papier-mâché, cardboard and tape from your demonstration goalie mask. Wash and dry the goalie mask so it can be used as a mold (or a goalie mask) in the future. The children's masks will need two to five days drying time before color can be added.

SECOND SESSION

Materials

- drop cloth or newspapers
- children's sculpted masks
- paints in assorted colors (Tempera paints are inexpensive and colorful, but they sometimes crack during the drying process. If this becomes a problem, mix a little white glue into each color to reduce cracking. Acrylic paints work well and won't crack, but are more expensive.)
- paintbrushes
- paper towels
- pad of inexpensive doodling paper
- felt-tip markers or colored pencils

Preparing the Work Area

1. Protect the work area with newspaper or drop cloths. If you left children's masks to dry on their original worktable, you are already prepared.

2. Place children's sculpted mask at their individual work spaces.

3. Place paints, brushes and paper towels in the center of the table where all can reach them.

4. Spread out doodling paper and markers or colored pencils on a neighboring table.

Completing the Second Part of the Project

1. Inform mask makers that today they will have the opportunity to add color to their masks. Point out the table with the paper and crayons, and let them know that they can use these materials to experiment with design and color options to plan their masks. Students may choose to try several different combinations on paper before they decide how they will paint their masks.

2. Children can paint their masks in whatever colors and patterns they want. Show them how to scrape excess paint off the brush by stroking it against the side of the paint container. Use paper towels to dab up any spills or drips.

3. Have children help put away the paints and clean the brushes. Allow at least one overnight for masks to dry before children can complete them.

THIRD SESSION

Materials

- 1/2"- to 1"-wide elastic (18" to 28" per mask)
- stapler
- scissors
- lightweight decorations such as yarn, feathers, glitter glue, crepe paper streamers, garlands, artificial flowers, ribbon, sequins, tinsel
- white household glue

Completing the Project

1. Before children add the final decorations to their masks, help them attach elastic support straps. Staple one end of a long piece of elastic near the outside edge of the mask at the level of the eyeholes. Have the child put the mask on. Pull the elastic around the back of the child's head over to the opposite edge of the mask, making a snug fit. Hold the elastic in position while the child removes the mask. Staple the elastic to the mask and cut off any surplus elastic.

If any of the masks seem loose or wobbly when worn, add a stabilizing strap of elastic. Attach one end of this elastic to the center of the top edge of the mask, and loop it over the top of the child's head and down to the original head strap at the center back of the head. Staple the straps together where they meet, forming a T-shape support system.

2. Point out the decorations and glue. Invite children to attach materials to their masks which they feel are appropriate to the masked personality they are creating (beards, hair, eyebrows, etc.). Allow time for the glue to dry before using the masks.

Using the Mask

This is a classic mask style which is visually interesting even when viewed from the side—especially if its facial features have been built up and exaggerated. If possible, give children a chance to practice their masked movements in front of a mirror. Since this mask does not interfere with body movement, students are free to practice various techniques. Encourage them to enlarge their movements, to slow them down, to freeze an action by holding an interesting pose, and to vary head and hand positions until they complement the mood suggested by a body position. Ask students to experiment with different walks until they find the one best suited to their masked character.

Variations

- Styrofoam can be a good lightweight material for adding underlying shape to this mask. Cut it into desired shapes with a steak knife, attach it to a papier-mâché foundation mask with masking tape, and cover it over with white newsprint papier-mâché before painting.

- Attach 12" x 12" sections of lightweight cloth or tissue paper to the top edge of the mask to cover the wearer's hair. Cut the bottom edges of this head covering into a hair-like fringe, or glue sections of crepe paper streamers to the cloth to simulate hair.

- Substitute inch-wide strips of poster board for the elastic head straps. These flexible cardboard straps provide a foundation for attaching yarn, cloth or paper hair.

- Tape strips of foam rubber about 6" long to the fingertips of rubber gloves. When the gloves are worn, the mask wearer will have an impressive looking

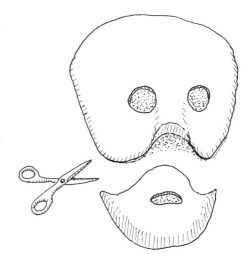

To make a speaking mask, cut the dried brown paper foundation layer into two pieces, with the dividing line between the nose and mouth. Discard the lower section, and continue with the other directions as described—ignoring references to the mouth slit.

but harmless set of long fingernails or claws.

• Adapt this mask into a speaking mask during its initial construction stage. Remove the papier-mâché mask from the goalie mask mold after the brown paper grocery bag layers have dried. Cut the eyeholes as directed. Now cut away and discard the bottom portion of the mask—the part which would cover the mouth and chin—but don't remove the part which covers the cheeks. Continue as directed. The mask wearer's mouth becomes the mouth of the mask. Mask wearers will be able to speak lines clearly and add limited facial expression to performances.

Shortcuts

• To cut down on required drying time, color papier-mâché masks with oil pastels instead of paint. Children can then decorate their masks during the same session in which they color them making this a two-session project for the children.

• Eliminate all of the papier-mâché work entirely—including its prep work—and still give children an opportunity to add sculpted features to their masks by trying the following super time-saver:

Prepare a Paper Plate Mask foundation for each child. Have children sculpt facial features using a modeling compound made by Crayola® called Model Magic™. Noses, lips and ears can be molded right onto the mask. This modeling compound is nontoxic, lightweight and pliable, and it will air dry in twenty-four hours. Insert decorative materials such as feathers, pipe cleaners, yarn, artificial flowers, beads and buttons into the modeling compound before it is dry, or glue them on afterward. After the modeling compound dries, color it with felt-tip markers, oil pastels, watercolors, tempera or acrylic paints. You can even apply colors with acrylic paints before the compound has dried. Such convenience has a price, of course, but this modeling material can be a better bargain if you buy it by the bucket instead of in individual packets.

PART THREE

SETTING THE STAGE

FIVE

What Was That Blurry Thing?

....

How to Make Your Puppets and Masks Come Alive

Maybe you've already tried making puppets with children, only to see the newly completed creations bop each other on the head incessantly or mumble indistinguishable dialogue while examining the ceiling.

How can you challenge children to use puppets and masks in a truly interesting and dramatic way—a way which helps tell a story?

Performance Guidelines for Children

- If lines are to be spoken by a performer, they should be spoken with enough volume to be heard on the other side of the room, especially if the performer is wearing a mask which covers the mouth. Explain to children that an audience creates a certain amount of noise. Performers' words will not be heard unless they are spoken at a volume louder than a normal speaking voice. It is also important to speak slowly. A rushed sentence sounds like a hissing radiator to an audience. Don't be afraid to inject a few dramatic pauses. With this advice in mind, performers can choose voices which they feel suit the character of their puppets or masks: shrill, soothing, commanding, cackling, dopey or quavering. Give students time to practice their speaking techniques.

- If several performers are on stage at the same time, they should try to remember to position themselves where they will not block the audience's view of the other performers.

- If the performers are using flat, two-dimensional masks or puppets, it is important that they try to keep the decorated sides facing the audience as much as possible.

OPERATING PUPPETS

Although puppets vary in style, size and maneuverability, several guidelines apply to all:

- As a general rule of thumb, only the puppet that is speaking should be moving. The supporting cast should be silent and still so the eyes of the audience will be drawn to the movement and it will be clear to them which character is speaking. There are certainly exceptions to this rule, times when several puppets need to be moving at once. But a lot of unnecessary background motion can be confusing to an audience.

- A puppet's movements will be more convincing if the puppeteer moves his or her body in a similar manner whenever possible. If the puppet is creeping along the top of the curtain, the puppeteer should be tiptoeing along below it. If the puppet is swaying and dancing about, the puppeteer should be too.

- Whenever a puppet speaks or moves, it should face the audience as much as possible. When the puppet speaks to another puppet standing at its side, it should turn its head only slightly in that direction. Some puppets lose dimension when they turn completely sideways; others, like High-Flying Bird or the Industrious Horse, are exceptions to this rule, since they have more substance when viewed from the side. Some puppets revert to odd pieces of unpainted cardboard when they turn their backs to an audience. This is often a difficult concept for children to remember. Seat the children together and demonstrate what happens when a two-dimensional puppet turns away from them.

- Suggest to puppeteers that they keep their eyes on their puppets as much as possible so they can see how their manipulations affect the puppets. Give children time to experiment with puppet movement. If possible, let them practice operating their puppets in front of a mirror. This will give them an idea what their performance will look like to the audience.

STORYTELLING WITH MASKS

Masks also come in infinite shapes and sizes. Some styles are designed for speaking performers, some are made for mimed performances. All are fascinating in their ability to transform their wearers into completely different characters.

These suggestions can help your students bring stories to life using masks:

- Encourage masked performers to exaggerate their movements, as this brings masks to life and makes characters more compelling. Remind students that masked performers cannot change their facial expressions, and must therefore rely on body language to communicate personalities and feelings. When children put on masks, they are free to explore the movements that their masked characters might make. They are no longer their everyday selves, they are playing a part.

- Seat the children together, and tell them you are going to give a demonstration in masked communication. Put on a simple generic-type mask, such as a Paper Plate Mask or an unadorned plastic hockey mask. Just stand there with your arms hanging at your sides for a few moments. Take off the mask. When you put the mask back on, move around the room using a combination of body postures and gestures which illustrate a human characteristic or personality trait. Make up your own combination of movements or try one of the following:

Perky and curious—Walk or skip with a lighthearted step. Cock your head while examining something. Peep into containers. Pick up an object and play with it.

Belligerent and blustering—Walk around in a determined fashion with your upper body leading the way. Swing your arms and shoulders with each step, with your arms bent at the elbow and your hands balled into fists. Point to an object and motion impatiently for someone to give it to you. Try to open the door but when you can't get it open shake your fists at the sky and stamp your foot.

Cautious and shy—Hold both hands in front of your face and peek out from behind them. Hang your head and shuffle forward while looking at the floor. Stop and lift your head slightly looking cautiously from side to side before dropping your head and shuffling slowly up to one of the children. Keep your head down while you hesitantly offer your hand to that child for a handshake.

Don't say anything during your masked demonstration. Use movement alone to communicate the personality of the masked character. After your demonstration, take off the mask and ask the children which performance was more interesting to watch. Which performance revealed more about the masked character? Which performance do they think would be the most interesting for a performer?

- Talk to the children about body language—how people communicate emotions through body position and movement. Ask them to show you without using words how people act when they are sad, happy, angry, shy, puzzled, nervous or excited. How do they hold their heads and shoulders? What do they do with their hands? How do they walk? Give students a chance to practice communicating some of these emotions while wearing their masks.

- Masked performers benefit enormously from the opportunity to practice in front of a large mirror, where they can study the effects they produce as they experiment with different styles of movement. If this is not possible, divide children into pairs or small groups and encourage them to experiment with different moves while providing feedback for each other.

- Encourage children to observe the use of body language on television, in movies and in their everyday life. How can they tell when their friends are excited? How can they tell when a parent is worried about something? Ask them to watch part of a dramatic television program with the sound turned off so they can focus on the performers' use of gesture and posture to express personality and emotions.

A NOTE ON PARADES

Parades offer a festive way to display children's puppet and mask creations. They can be organized around a story, event or holiday, and they offer a perfect vehicle for exploring cultural variety. Make a parade a classroom project or involve the whole school, each classroom making puppets, masks or animated scenery representing a different country, culture or book. Plan a community parade designed to give children an opportunity to meet and work with other children in their community and as a means of encouraging families to participate in a school-community project.

Ask children to devise sound effects and simple musical instruments to add dash and liveliness to the festivities. Parent, teacher and student musicians might also lend their talents to the project. Parades are an excellent showcase for large puppets, which are most effective when interspersed among smaller creations.

A bunched-up parade becomes a cluttered mass of arms and legs. To save your parade from this tangled fate, caution participants to move forward slowly and allow a little empty space behind the person they follow. This will ensure that every puppet and masked character will have room to perform and that the audience will be able to see everything clearly.

If paraders are divided into groups, leave a noticeable space gap between each group to discourage crowding. Appoint a person at the front of each group to be the spacer.

If the weather is cooperative, stage the parade outside. School hallways, cafeterias and gymnasiums can provide parading space on rainy days.

SIX

Scenery in Motion

....

Would the Thundercloud on the Right Please Tie Her Shoelaces?

You have a group of children eager to experience the creative excitement of dramatic storytelling, but you have a little problem with numbers. You've just combed through three books of folk and fairy tales and have discovered that most of these stories feature only a handful of characters. You need a story with enough acting parts for fifty children. What can you do?

Think scenery!

But don't think of scenery in the traditional sense—a mere a painted backdrop for the real action. Imagine interactive scenery: dynamic scenery which children can carry about a room and manipulate with interpretive actions; scenery which can be used to convey the graceful flow of time or the exciting threat of a storm; scenery which actively helps tell a story.

Is there a thunderstorm in your story? Imagine ten children boiling out from behind a curtain shaking home-made thunderclouds to produce rumbling sound effects. Does a flood threaten the village? Cardboard waves roll in, trailing crepe paper streamers as the shimmering cloth river rises higher and higher. Does the plot develop over a period of time? A fluorescent sun, a ghostly moon and a scattering of gently jingling stars glide above the curtain to set the scene and charm the audience. Not only can interactive scenery solve your numbers problem, it can add a captivating beauty to the children's dramatizations.

Once you begin to think in terms of active scenery, scenery that swoops and swirls and shimmies, you will begin to seek out stories offering plum parts for clouds, waves and the hypnotic tokens of time. The children who manipulate this type of mobile scenery will often be performing in front of the curtain and will therefore be in clear view of the audience. Don't let this worry you. The children will have greater freedom of movement, and the results will be captivating. If the children concentrate on moving their scenery in an interesting manner, in a way which captures the spirit of the object they are portraying, the attention of the audience will be drawn to the active scenery and their view of the performer will not be distracting but will provide additional charm to the performance. If you would like to heighten this contrast even further, ask those performers who will be in full view of the audience to dress in plain dark clothing. The unadorned clothing will fade into the background, and the colorful movement of the scenery and puppets will be further emphasized.

The scenery described in this chapter requires very little preparation time on the part of the assisting adult. It's mostly a matter of gathering materials together so children can work with them.

Flamboyant Sun

This bright and colorful piece of scenery rises majestically into the air, its bright countenance signaling another day for the characters in your story.

Materials

- 22" x 28" sheet of white poster board
- oil pastels or crayons in assorted bright, warm colors
- scissors
- construction paper and crepe paper streamers in warm colors (red, yellow, orange, pink) Neon colors are especially effective.
- white household glue
- flat wooden control rod 2' to 3' long (See Chapter 1 for suggestions.)
- duct tape

Construction

1. The child who will operate the sun can use pastels or crayons to draw a sun on the full sheet of poster board. Encourage the artist to make an impressively large sun, reaching all the way out to the edges of the poster board—a sun whose shimmering image will dance in the audience's eye. Once the coloring is complete, cut away any surplus poster board.

2. Cut construction paper into triangular rays and glue them to the sun's edges. The artist may want to try cutting the construction paper into narrow strips, bending the strips into accordion folds and attaching one end of each strip to the surface of the sun. These colorful zigzags will reach out from the sun and vibrate like waves of heat. Crepe paper streamers can be cut and attached as rays of sunlight.

3. Help the child glue the control rod to the back of the sun. Make sure the rod overlaps the back of the sun for most of its height, as this stiffens the poster board and prevents the top of the sun from flopping over. Reinforce the control rod attachment with duct tape.

Animating the Scenery

With the help of its control rod, the sun can be made to rise slowly from behind one end of the curtain, sail grandly across its top and sink gracefully out of sight behind the curtain's other end. Or the child might hold the sun up (with its decorated side facing the audience) as he or she enters from one side of the curtain, glides slowly across its front with a sliding sideways step and exits behind the curtain's other side. Encourage the puppeteer to experiment with different manipulation techniques: varying the speed of movement, vibrating the control rod, using larger or smaller steps. Explore different sound effects till one is found that enhances the sun's presence. (See Chapter 8.)

Variations

- If you can allow for additional drying time, use tempera paints to decorate the sun.

- Glue small pieces of metallic paper and mirror-like sequins to the sun to produce scattered sparkles of reflected light.

Shortcut

- Cut a large circle out of poster board and attach a control rod with glue and duct tape. Present this prefab orb to the child, who can develop it into a more individualized sun with the materials suggested previously. Make sure the young artist has enough space to work on the sun without accidentally poking a neighboring child with the attached control rod.

Drifting Moon

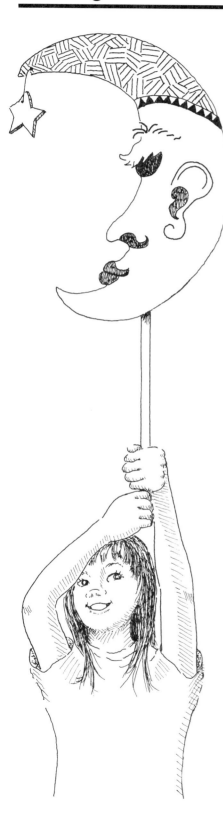

The moon is a graceful alter ego to the sun, helping to mark the passage of time and setting the scene for a story's nighttime episode. It is especially effective if accompanied by a few singing stars, described later in this chapter.

Materials

- 22" x 28" sheet of white poster board
- crayons in assorted shadowy colors such as blue, purple, gray, black (A silver metallic crayon is a great option.)
- scissors
- glitter glue (blue, silver, purple, white)
- flat wooden control rod 2' to 3' long (See Chapter 1 for suggestions.)
- white household glue
- duct tape

Construction

1. Encourage the artist to draw his or her version of the moon, making it as large as the poster board will allow. It could be a curving crescent moon, a great round full moon, or a yin-yang moon with one half light and the other half dark. Add crater shadows or fanciful facial features. Once the moon is complete, cut away excess poster board.

2. Decorate the moon as desired with glitter glue.

3. Once the glitter glue is dry, attach the control stick as described in step three of the instructions for the Flamboyant Sun.

Animating the Scenery

The moon is most effective if moved in a slow and graceful manner, floating elegantly through the air. Its visual effect can be greatly enhanced if it is accompanied by a simple, haunting sound effect (See Chapter 8). The decorated side of the moon should always face the audience.

Variation

- Obtain a haunting effect by decorating the moon with glow-in-the-dark paints. The room will have to be darkened to achieve the intended results, but the floating glowing presence you create will be a stunner!

Shortcut

- If time is short, attach the control rod in advance. Cut a full moon or crescent out of poster board and attach the control rod with glue and duct tape. The child can develop it with the materials suggested. Make sure that the student has enough space to work on the moon without poking a neighbor with the control rod.

Tumultuous Thundercloud

This thundercloud is a lot of fun and provides its own sound effect. Several dark clouds rumbling and rolling across the room together create a greater dramatic effect than one little cloud grumbling to itself as it wanders about, so plan to have three or more children make thunderclouds if your story calls for a storm.

Materials

- 22" x 28" sheet of white poster board (one per puppet)
- children's scissors
- crayons or oil pastels (blue, black, green, gray, purple, yellow)
- aluminum foil
- clear plastic tape
- white household glue
- pipe cleaners (two per puppet)
- duct tape

Construction

1. Have the children use scissors to shape the poster board sheets into big lumpy cloud shapes; cutting the corner points off is a good start. Instruct them to use crayons or oil pastels to turn their clouds into dark, threatening storm clouds. Paper can be peeled away from the crayons and oil pastels so the sides can be used to make wide, sweeping strokes of color. Add yellow streaks of lightning.

2. Cut the aluminum foil into strips, and attach them to the bottom edge of each cloud with clear plastic tape or glue. These strips will simulate streaks of rain and contribute to the sound effects.

3. Once the clouds are complete, turn them over. Position the two pipe cleaners on the back of each poster board so that they are parallel to the side edges of the cloud and about 1' apart (the child will operate the cloud by holding one pipe cleaner handle in each hand). Tape both ends of each pipe cleaner securely to the poster board with duct tape, leaving a little arched slack in the middle of each pipe cleaner so it can be grasped easily.

Animating the Scenery

The children hold the clouds out in front of their bodies, a handle in each hand. If they shake the clouds back and forth rapidly, the poster boards will produce a satisfying rumbling sound, the silvery rain streaks will wave wildly about—and the audience will begin to pull their collars about their necks in anticipation of a soaking.

Variations

- Transform a large black plastic trash bag into a simple costume for each thundercloud operator. Cut off both bottom corners for armholes, and cut a V shape out of the middle of the bag's bottom edge for a head hole. Slip the open end of the bag over the child's head and help slide the arms and head into the openings you made. The bag becomes a black rustling tunic—the perfect garment for a thundercloud operator. Glue strips of aluminum foil onto its front in zigzag lightning patterns.

- If your story calls for peaceful floating clouds, have the children use chalk or pastel colored crayons to decorate their clouds. Glue cotton balls and slightly crumpled tissue paper in soft colors to the poster board to add dimension to the clouds.

- Make clouds out of sturdy cardboard, and glue a control rod onto the back for a high floating cloud which can tower over your curtain from behind. While impressive to look at, this type of cloud will not have a built-in sound effect, so you may want to have a sound effects person with a thunder sheet (See Chapter 8) to supply this missing element.

Shortcut

- Thunderclouds can be made more quickly by starting with black poster board; simply round off the corners and add foil rain and pipe cleaner handles.

Singing Stars

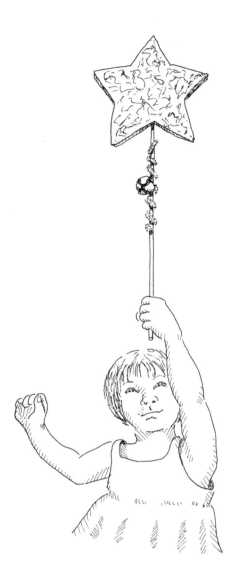

Sparkling prettily and accompanied by their own built-in sound effects, a scattering of stars can appear to set the stage for a night scene. These stars make attractive companions for the moon.

Materials

- felt-tip markers
- plain, flexible white paper plate or piece of thin cardboard (one per star)
- children's scissors
- white household glue
- aluminum foil or metallic wrapping paper
- pipe cleaner (one per star)
- small jingle bells with metal loops (one or more per star)
- thin control rod 2' to 3' long, such as a thin wooden dowel or bamboo plant stake (one per star)
- masking tape

Construction

1. Using a felt-tip marker, ask each child to draw a large star on a paper plate. If any of the children have trouble drawing a star, you might suggest that they first draw a circle or a square, then draw triangular points around this central shape.

2. Have children cut out their stars.

3. Apply small dabs of glue to the top surface of each cardboard star. Turn the star over and press the glued surface against a sheet of aluminum foil or metallic wrapping paper; make sure the foil covers the entire glued surface of the star. Cut away any surplus aluminum foil. The stars will now have one side with a shiny surface.

4. Tell the children to thread a pipe cleaner through the loop of one or more bells.

5. Help the students attach one end of the control rod to the back side of the star (the side without the foil) using a couple of strips of masking tape. Wrap the jingling pipe cleaner around the control rod just below the star.

Animating the Scenery

The children use the control rods to hold the twinkling stars high above their heads. The stars can pop up from behind a curtain or can be paraded slowly across its front. A slight up-and-down movement of the rod or a twisting of the wrist will set the bells jingling.

Variation

- Instead of decorating with aluminum foil, paint the stars or color them with metallic crayons. Use glitter glue to provide the twinkle.

Flowing River

This simple piece of moving scenery can be developed and operated by two or three children. The river has many advantageous features: it adds an element of graceful swaying movement to any dramatization, it can double as a portable curtain for water-dwelling puppets (See *Why Fish Can't Sing* in Chapter 9) and it can also be used to represent an ocean, lake or wandering stream.

Materials

- piece of blue cloth roughly 1 yard x 3 yards (This river-as-puppet curtain is particularly effective if the cloth is lightweight and translucent.)
- oil pastels in assorted colors
- 4" to 8" lengths of yarn
- white household glue
- lightweight decorations such as sequins, small pieces of reflective paper, glitter

Construction

1. Spread the cloth out flat on the floor so children can draw on it with colored pastels. Before students begin to decorate the material, let them decide which of the long edges will be the surface or top of the water. Ask them to think about how water looks when it moves in the wind and glimmers with reflected sunlight. What kind of animals and plants live in the water? Encourage the children to draw those things on the cloth.

2. When students have finished with the pastels, make available the yarn, glue and lightweight decorations. Attach the decorations to the cloth with small dabs of glue to simulate ripples and glittering reflections. Allow the glue to dry before moving the cloth.

Animating the Scenery

The children who will operate the river simply grab a bit of the cloth's top edge in each hand and hold the material so it hangs down in front of them. One child should be at either end of the cloth, with a third child supporting the middle, if desired. Students should practice holding the cloth so that the decorated side is always facing the audience. Have them practice moving their hands forward and back so that the cloth sways and flows. Direct them to move sideways together across the room in a serpentine pattern while gently swishing the cloth back and forth in front of them. If the river is going to make an appearance partway through a story dramatization, provide the children with a waiting place where they can sit side-by-side on chairs or on the floor while holding onto the top edge of the river—ready to leap into action without having to pause to untangle the river cloth.

Variation

• Let the children draw water creatures on construction paper, cut them out and attach them to the cloth.

• Have the children who make the river each make a Paper Plate Mask to wear while operating the river. The children could decorate their masks with watercolors or felt-tip markers in abstract water designs such as ripples, flowing lines and swirls.

Walking Wave

This handy piece of scenery can double as a portable curtain if your story features small rod puppets who swim, sail or simply float about. The wave can be operated by one child.

Materials

• 22" x 28" sheet of white poster board (one piece per puppet)
• oil pastels or crayons in assorted blues and greens
• children's scissors
• tissue paper (one full-size sheet of blue or green tissue paper per wave, and several smaller pieces of green, blue, and white tissue paper)
• glue stick
• pipe cleaners (two per wave)
• duct tape

Construction

1. The children who are making the waves should each draw a curving line representing a cresting wave just below one of the long edges of their poster board. Have them cut along this line with scissors and decorate the poster boards in designs which convey the feeling of swirling, rolling water. Peel the paper from the crayons and pastels so they can be used sideways to obtain a wider line. Show the children how to tear the smaller pieces of tissue paper into thin, undulating shapes and use the glue stick to layer these right over the colored poster board to represent the transparent swirls of color in moving water.

2. Once the waves are complete, attach two pipe cleaner handles to the back of each with duct tape. Position the two pipe cleaners on the back of the poster board so they are parallel to the side edges of the poster board and about 2' apart. The child will support the wave by holding one handle in each hand. Attach both ends of each pipe cleaner securely to the poster board with duct tape, leaving a little arched slack in the middle of each pipe cleaner so it can be grasped easily.

3. Attach one edge of a full-size tissue paper sheet to the bottom back-side edge of the poster board (the uncut long edge). This sheet of tissue paper should hang freely from the bottom of the wave.

Animating the Scenery

The wave operator holds the wave in front of his or her body and walks out slowly with the decorated side facing the audience. The tissue paper sheet will help hide the wave handler's legs. The wave can be rocked slightly from side to side or moved in rolling undulations. If small rod puppets will be used with the wave, these puppeteers can walk out behind the wave handler, keeping their puppets close to their bodies until it is time for them to pop up from behind the wave.

The wave is operated by two pipe cleaner handles, like the Tumultuous Thundercloud, or by a flat wooden control rod taped to its back.

Variations

- Cut the wave from a sheet of sturdy cardboard to create a stiffer version.

- Smaller, more mobile waves can be made from large, round paper plates; cardboard pizza plates work great, if you can talk your local pizza parlor into parting with a few. Using blue and green oil pastels, the children can turn the plate bottoms into spheres of watery swirls. Loosely wad up white tissue paper and glue it here and there on the plate bottoms to simulate foam. Glue yard-long ribbons of crepe paper streamers to the plate edges. Students hold the paper plate waves out in front of their bodies with the decorated sides facing out. As they flow into the audience's view, they swirl their plates in a circular motion, causing the crepe paper ribbons to weave a watery dance.

Use cardboard pizza plates or large, stiff paper plates to produce a clashing swirl of small mobile waves.

Wandering Mountain

Make a do-it-yourself mountain range complete with three snowy peaks. This three-person mountain can hitch up its skirts and walk to whatever location will best serve your storytelling needs—but don't be surprised if it is occasionally beset by an avalanche of giggles.

Materials

- **piece of white cloth, at least 7' x 9' (A queen-size flat sheet works great!)**
- **sharp scissors**
- **felt-tip markers in assorted colors**
- **three half pieces of white poster board (each half piece should measure 22" x 14")**
- **three 15" lengths of 1/2" elastic**
- **stapler**

Construction

1. Spread the sheet out on the floor. The assisting adult can cut three random holes in the cloth, with each hole at least 3' from the edge of the cloth and 2' or 3' distant from the other holes. Make each hole about 7" across (large enough for a child's head to slide through).

Once the holes have been cut, the children can decorate the cloth with felt-tip markers. Let them try on the cloth, and point out that each hole marks the upper slopes of a mountain. The straight edges of the cloth mark the bottoms of the mountains. Ask students what they see when they close their eyes and think of mountains: Trees? Rocks? Rushing streams? Give children time to draw these images on the outspread cloth.

2. While students are decorating the cloth, the assisting adult can roll each piece of poster board into a cone hat: Starting with a 14" edge, roll the poster board into a fairly tight tube. Keep one hand around one end of the tube to keep it tight while you use your other hand to spread the other end open until it can fit over a child's head. Staple it to secure its shape. Cut off any dangling tails if you prefer a smooth cone shape.

Place this snow-capped mountain peak upon the head of one of the children. Staple an elastic chin strap to the hat on both sides just in front of the ears, adjusting its length so it will keep the hat on with a comfortable amount of tension. Repeat with the other two pieces of poster board. As each child's hat is completed, the student can decorate its outside surface with a little alpine scenery.

Animating the Scenery

The children who are to wear the mountain should stand together while the assisting adult drapes the cloth over them, fitting each child's head through one of the holes. Students should stand a little distance apart and hold hands so that the fabric will drape loosely over the mountain's separate peaks. Top each mountain with a decorated cone hat.

When they are in position, let the children practice holding their arms in different positions to see how it affects the shape of their mountain range.

Variations

• Decorate the mountain cloth and hats with tempera paint. Allow for drying time.

• Cut out trees and rocks from construction paper and attach them to the cloth and cone hats with glue or tape.

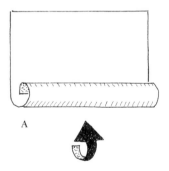

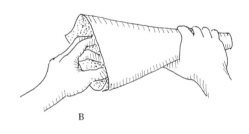

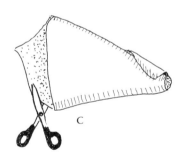

Create a cone-shape mountaintop hat for each child in your mountain range.

Poster Board Garden

Plop a sheet of poster board on the floor, slap on some construction paper vegetables—presto, instant garden! Such a garden comes in handy when dramatizing such stories as *The Ogre's Staircase* (See Chapter 9).

Materials

- 22" x 28" sheet of poster board or large flat piece of sturdy cardboard
- construction paper or scraps of poster board
- children's scissors
- felt-tip markers in assorted colors
- clear plastic tape

Construction

1. Lay a sheet of poster board on the floor, with construction paper, scissors, tape and felt-tip markers nearby.

2. Have children draw, decorate and cut out assorted paper vegetables. Fold these vegetables once horizontally across the middle, and tape their bottom halves to the poster board or a sheet of sturdy cardboard. The top half of each vegetable should stick up in the air as if the plant were growing out of the ground.

Animating the Scenery

Actually, this garden does not dance, sing or emote. It is a colorful bit of lightweight stationary scenery whose construction makes for an enjoyable group activity.

Shimmering Tree

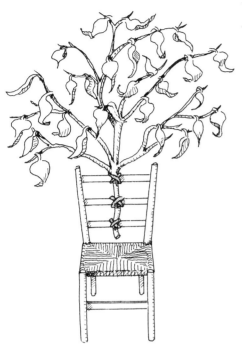

Not the sort of tree you'd see on your average stroll through the woods, this eye-catching species makes a great group project.

Materials

- **leafless, branching tree branch**
- **masking tape**
- **chair**
- **aluminum foil or colorful wrapping paper**
- **children's scissors**
- **pictures showing various leaf shapes (optional)**
- **clear plastic tape**

Construction

1. Secure the tree branch to the back of a chair with masking tape.

2. Children can cut or tear different leaf shapes from the foil or wrapping paper. (Displayed pictures of a variety of leaf shapes would be helpful.) They should give each leaf a long stem, so the end can be attached to the tree branch with clear plastic tape.

Animating the Scenery

Leave the tree taped to the chair and place it where it will serve as scenery for your story. If you are using the tree to help tell the story *Why Fish Can't Sing* (Chapter 9), appoint a child to reach out and shake the branch so that a papery rustling sound can be heard as the leaves brush against each other. If you are dramatizing the story *The Ogre's Staircase* (Chapter 9), the children can create a small enchanted forest of these trees.

As an alternative, release the tree from its chair and ask a child to hold it. Make sure the child understands the need to keep the branch well away from people's faces.

Variations

- Use brightly colored cellophane to make very attractive and suitably noisy leaves.

- Drape the chair with a piece of green cloth, transforming it into a lumpy hillside crowned with a great spreading tree.

SEVEN

Stages for Storytelling

....

There Just Isn't Room for the Ten of Us in This Refrigerator Box!

(Opposite) **Most homemade stages are unable to handle a large cast of characters.**

Let's say you've been working with a group of children on a story-telling arts project. They've made a delightful cast of puppets, masks and active scenery and are eager to dramatize a story. What can you use for a stage?

The traditionally small, enclosed puppet theater provides space for no more than one or two sedate puppeteers. Anymore than that and you are inviting a pandemonium of poked eyes, squashed feet and flattened puppets. This chapter will suggest several user-friendly alternatives—stages that are easy to construct, inexpensive and capable of accommodating a classroom of enthusiastic puppeteers.

These are not the usual self-contained stages with a split curtain to pull open and closed, and the puppeteers who use these stages are not always stuffed away out of sight. These are multi-purpose stages which offer children plenty of room to explore and develop interpretive movements. They consist of centrally located decorated curtains, easily accessible to performers at the front, back and sides, which encourage full use of adjacent performance space. Performers who are not yet on stage can hide behind the curtain—puppets can appear from its top, sides and bottom—and it becomes a scenic backdrop for those who perform in front of it. A menacing ogre can glare out at the audience over the top of the curtain before lumbering out in front of it to scatter the chickens who have been pecking industriously at the floor by the audience's feet. Colorful butterflies can drift quietly out from behind one side of the curtain, flap gracefully across its painted woodland scene and gently disappear behind its other edge. The children are often in plain view, but their puppets, masks and active scenery still manage to steal the show!

These stages can be used in many ways. Be inventive; use a mixture of large and small puppets, masked performers and interactive scenery. They can all work together to dramatize your story. Don't be limited to the space behind the central curtain. Performers can use the area in front of it and on both sides as well. The variety will add visual appeal to your performance.

Decorating the Stage

All the stages described in this book feature some type of cloth or paper curtain. Preparing one provides an excellent opportunity for a group art activity. When children make their puppets, masks and active scenery, they can also decorate the curtain with backdrop scenery appropriate to the story they are about to enact. Their decorations will show up more effectively if you give them a white or light-colored curtain to embellish.

Scenery can be added to the curtain before it is attached to its support system. Spread the cloth or paper out on the floor, designate one of the long edges as the top and give children time to transform it into a colorful landscape. Students can draw directly on the cloth with felt-tip markers, oil pastels, chalk, crayons, or tempera paints. (Protect the floor with a drop cloth or newspaper if using paints.) Or they can draw trees, rocks, houses, etc. on construction paper, cut them out and attach them to the curtain with clear plastic tape or folded double-stick masking tape (See "Masking tape" in "What Materials to Use," in Chapter 1). If students use washable felt-tip markers or construction paper to decorate the curtain, the cloth can be reused later for another story; the felt-tip markers will wash out, and the construction paper and tape can be removed.

If possible, give children the opportunity to look at pictures illustrating the local color of the story they will be dramatizing (plants, animals, architecture, etc.) before they begin to decorate the curtain. Pictures showing the costumes and customs of different countries can be found in libraries. These visual aids provide children with a chance to learn about other cultures as they work on their creative arts project. Display these pictures in a prominent place so students can refer to them as they work.

Rope Curtain Stage

Once prepared, this curtain can be set up and taken down quickly and can be stored in a grocery bag. If you have a couple of conveniently spaced trees to support the rope ends, it can easily become an outdoor stage.

Materials

- thin strong rope (clothesline works fine)
- white flat sheet, or similar large piece of cloth
- spring-type clothespins, duct tape or safety pins
- two sturdy hooks, screw eyes or large nails (optional)

Construction

Attach the rope at both ends so it stretches across the full width of the room or across a large corner portion of it. You can usually find two secure supports for the rope, such as sturdy coat hooks or wall-based flag holders. You could tie a big knot at one end of the rope, open an upper window from the top, push the knot through and close the window, or push the knot over the top of a closet door and shut it firmly. If you cannot find two convenient anchors, you may have to purchase two sturdy hooks or screw eyes to attach to wooden window or door frames. Another alternative is to pound two large nails into a wooden surface at an angle. Once the rope is in position, adjust the amount of slack until the rope's center section hangs at a level slightly above the tops of the children's heads. Drape the cloth over the center section of rope so that it hangs to the floor in front. Secure the cloth with clothespins, duct tape or safety pins.

Using the Stage

Some children can stand in back of the curtain, with their puppets making their appearances over its top. Some puppets can poke up from the bottom of the cloth or project out at different heights along its sides. The area in front of the curtain is also an excellent performance space. Active scenery can appear from behind the curtain, perform in front of it or cross from one side of the room to the other. Large puppets will have more room to move if they make use of the performance space in front of the curtain. Masked performers can step out in front of the curtain so their interpretive body movements can be seen clearly. Performers in front of the curtain can interact with puppets appearing from behind the curtain.

Children who are not operating their puppets can sit in chairs or on the floor several feet behind the curtain or along the sides of the room until it is time for their puppets to perform.

Large rod puppets may get snagged by the rope if they try to move from the area in back of the curtain to the performing space at its front. It would be easier for these puppeteers if they limited their performance area to either the front or back of the curtain. They could, for example, make their appearance from a doorway or a waiting area off to the side of the room and perform in front of the curtain, or loom up from behind it.

Table Stage

This simple stage, ideal for small and medium-size puppets, can be set up in a matter of minutes. You can use this stage to dramatize *Why Fish Can't Sing* (See Chapter 9).

Materials

- **long table**
- **large piece of cloth or roll of paper (long enough to stretch the length of the table and at least wide enough to cover the tabletop and extend down to the floor across the front)**
- **duct tape**

Construction

Drape the cloth or paper along one of the long sides of the table so it hangs down to the floor. Secure it to the top of the table with duct tape. If you have surplus cloth, wrap it around the short sides of the table or drape it over the tabletop.

Using the Stage

Children can crouch, kneel or sit on the floor behind the table, holding their puppets up above the tabletop and facing them out toward their audience. Active scenery can come from the side of the room and perform while crossing in front of the curtain. Masked performers can stand up tall to perform from behind the table, in front of it or while standing off to one side.

Variation

If a longer curtain is desired, push two or more tables together forming one long table, and attach the curtain to their combined length. You may need to use several pieces of cloth or paper, overlapping them slightly where they join. If long tables are not available, attach the curtain to a row of desks pushed together to form a solid line or to a row of sturdy chairs lined up with their backs facing the audience.

Ladder Curtain Stage

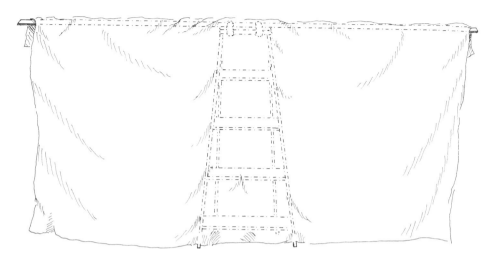

If you have access to a stepladder, you can easily construct this sturdy stage. Because it uses the ladder for its support, it already has built-in steps. This makes it ideal for enacting *The Ogre's Staircase* (See Chapter 9). It has no overhead rope supports to interfere with free passage of large rod puppets, but the ladder legs do steal a little of the performing space behind the curtain.

Materials

- stepladder (Ideally, the stepladder should be only slightly higher than the height of the performers who will be using the curtain. Stepladders can usually be found in heights of 3', 4', 5', 6' and 8'.)
- sturdy crossbar about 7' or 8' long (wooden pole, stiff flat rod or PVC plastic pipe with a 1" or 1 1/4" diameter)
- duct tape
- flat white bed sheet full-size or larger

Construction

Place the stepladder in the performing space with the steps facing out toward the audience. Lay the crossbar across the top of the ladder so it is parallel to the floor, and secure it in this position with duct tape. If the ladder is more than a few inches taller than the performers, tape the crossbar across one of the ladder's steps or lash it to the ladder's legs.

Drape the bed sheet curtain over the crossbar and any parts of the ladder which stick up above the crossbar. Secure it in this position with duct tape.

Using the Stage

Puppets can appear at the top, sides and bottom of this curtain. The floor space in front of the curtain provides additional performance space for large puppets and active scenery. Small puppets or props can be stored under the stepladder when not in use, safe from trampling feet.

If your crossbar is placed at a level below the top of the ladder, the sheet-covered bulge of the ladder top could be decorated to resemble a mountain, cloud, treetop or other bulky type of scenery.

Freestanding Curtain

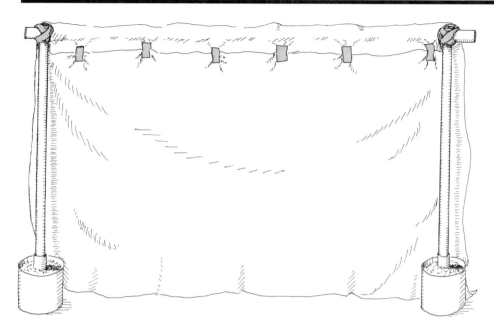

This curtain takes a bit longer to make, but it has several advantages. It has no projecting ropes or ladder legs to interfere with performance space, it can be set up just about anywhere, and it can be dismantled and stored in a corner when not in use. If you plan to use your stage frequently, the freestanding curtain is well worth your time.

Backstage view of Freestanding Curtain

Materials

- plastic wrap
- two pieces of 1 1/2"-diameter PVC pipe, each 1' long
- two strong rubber bands
- duct tape
- two small broad-bottomed buckets, 5- or 6-quart size
- drop cloth
- disposable work gloves
- cement mix (enough to fill both buckets with cement)
- sturdy container for mixing cement
- plumb line (A 2' length of string with one end tied to a heavy nut makes a handy homemade plumb line.)
- three pieces of 1 1/4"-diameter PVC plastic pipe, one piece cut 8' long for a crossbar, two pieces cut 5' long for

side poles (If the puppeteers are more than 5' tall, you will need longer side poles, as the side poles should be slightly taller than the performers.)
- two strips of cloth strapping or 1" wide elastic, each about 3' long (optional)
- white, flat bed sheet, twin-size or larger

Construction

Place plastic wrap over one end of 1' length of 1 1/2" PVC pipe and secure it with a rubber band. Close off the other end of the pipe with duct tape. Repeat this process with the other 1' section of pipe.

Set the buckets out on a drop cloth in a work area with a level floor. Stand one of the two short pipe sections on end in the middle of each bucket, with the duct-taped end on the bottom and the plastic-wrapped end sticking out. Put on work gloves; working cement with your bare hands will endow them with a memorable sandpaper texture. Mix the cement according to directions. If possible, ask someone to steady the pipes while you pour the fresh cement into both buckets. If you are working alone, steady each pipe with one hand while you use an empty

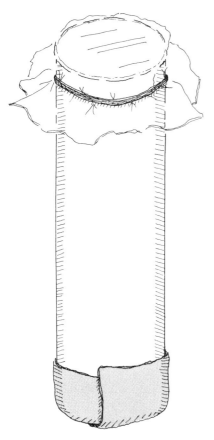

Cover one end of the 1' PVC pipe with plastic wrap, the other end with duct tape.

metal can to ladle cement into each bucket with the other hand. Add enough cement around the pipes so the mixture nearly fills each bucket but does not reach the plastic wrap on the top ends of the pipes. *Make sure no cement gets inside the pipes.*

Once the cement has been poured into the buckets—but before it has hardened—remove the rubber bands and plastic wrap. Drop the weighted end of your plumb line a few inches down into one of the pipes. Make sure the pipe is lined up straight with the hanging string. If not, the pipe is at an angle and needs to be gently repositioned until it lines up with the plumb line. Check the other pipe with the plumb line and straighten if necessary. Allow the cement to dry.

Place the buckets about 7 1/2' apart on the floor of your performance space. Put one end of a 5' side pole into each of the short pipe pieces embedded in cement; the poles should slide right into these short pipe sleeves, which have a larger diameter. The crossbar can then be attached to the side poles at a height slightly higher than the performers' heads and parallel to the floor. Wrap duct tape around the junctions of the crossbar and side poles to secure them. For easier dismantling, secure the crossbar to the side poles with cloth strapping or 1" straps of elastic instead of duct tape, and tie them off with a bow. Once you have found a good height for your crossbar, mark the desired height on the side poles so you can put the freestanding curtain

Use a homemade plumb line to make sure each short section of pipe is vertical before the cement hardens.

together more quickly next time you use it.

Drape the bed sheet over the crossbar and secure it with duct tape or safety pins. Let the performance begin!

Using the Stage

This curtain offers the largest number of options for unencumbered performance space. Puppets can make their appearance from the top, sides or bottom of the curtain. Large puppets or moving scenery can come out from behind the curtain or from the sides of the room and perform in the space in front of the curtain or on either side of it. Performers can move freely around this curtain without getting tangled in ropes or ladders.

If desired, a slit can be cut into the curtain from floor to crossbar at the halfway point, and masked performers can come through this opening to perform in front of the curtain.

You can also cut U-shape flaps into the curtain so that small hand puppets can poke their heads and bodies out to speak their lines. When the puppet withdraws, the flap falls back into its former position and closes the hole. If the area of cloth around each flap is decorated to look like a house or thatched hut, these puppets will look as if they are speaking from the doorways of their homes.

When the performance is over, the curtain, crossbar and side poles can be removed and stored in a corner of the room. The children can help you roll the cement-filled buckets to a convenient storage spot.

EIGHT

Sound Effects

....

*How a Pan Lid and a Screwdriver
Can Take You to the Orient*

Several members of your group can be responsible for providing sound effects to heighten
the dramatic effect of the storytelling performance.

The tinkling of distant bells draws the eyes of the audience to the glittering foil stars sinking slowly out of sight behind the curtain. Suddenly the very air vibrates when a cymbal's crescendo welcomes the broadly grinning face of the rising sun.

Sound effects can add a whole new dimension to your storytelling skills. A few simple sounds can weave a captivating auditory texture into the visual charms of a dramatic production. Sound effects can help cast the storyteller's spell over the audience—alerting it to the arrival of a new character, heightening the excitement of a dramatic confrontation or adding to the charm of a story's softly magical moments.

Sound effects also weave their spell over the performers—focusing them, cueing them and freeing them from excessive self-consciousness so they can become involved more fully in the story and its characters.

All these benefits aside, sound effects are fun! You and the children will enjoy experimenting with them. Collect an assortment of sound effects and spend some time testing their possibilities, discussing the emotions they evoke and choosing a program of sound effects to complement your dramatization. Ask the children: What sound should we choose to announce the arrival of the gentle giraffe? How do we accompany the sudden and threatening appearance of the dreadful ogre? Which of these sounds best suits the arrival of the sun after the terrible thunderstorm?

Explore the possibilities of sound inherent in common household objects. When the lion trots out, do you think a vegetable grater should be stroked slowly like this? Or should a series of quick, repetitive strokes like this be used?

Children will enjoy discovering new sound effects to add to this chapter's list of possibilities. They will also enjoy helping choose and produce sound effects accompaniments for their dramatic storytelling activities.

Gathering Sound Effects for Your Dramatizations

Many things for making sound effects can be found around the house, inexpensively purchased or easily constructed. Try them out. Experiment to see what different sounds can be produced. Discover new sound effects of your own. Keep your ears open for possibilities. Any musical instrument can be used to produce interesting sounds even if you do not know how to play a tune on it.

Once you have gathered your sound effects, dump them into a sturdy canvas bag or large plastic bucket. You now have a handy sound effects kit which can be hauled out whenever needed.

HOUSEHOLD OBJECTS

- Scrape a vegetable grater with the edge of a metal spoon. Try varying the rhythm and speed.

- Blow across the top of an open plastic soda pop bottle. You may have to experiment a little to get the angle right, but you will be rewarded with a satisfying hooting sound. Vary the pitch by adding different amounts of fluid to the bottle.

- Turn over a bucket, trash can or large metal tin, and drum on its bottom with your hands or a wooden spoon. Hold an empty metal can or a bowl made out of metal or wood upside down in one hand while you drum on its bottom with a chopstick or spoon. Try different combinations and rhythms until you find a pattern of drumbeats which sounds right to you. Drums can be used effectively to highlight a surprising entrance or to sustain an exciting development in the story action.

- Broiling pans, heavy pan lids, metal bowls and cooking pans can act as gongs, especially if they are made of brass, iron or steel. Attach a loop of strong string or shoelace and lift the pans into the air by the loop. Hit the metal with a large metal spoon or screwdriver. You will be rewarded with an impressive vibrating note.

- Clang two pan lids together as homemade cymbals. Experiment until you find two lids with a satisfying sound.

- Two flat, smooth oblong rocks can be hit together. The resulting sound will be more effective if you hold the rocks with the tips of your fingers so the sound is not muffled by the palms of your hands.

- A thin section of sheet metal, a flat section of fiberglass panel or a full sheet of poster board can make a good thunder sheet. Use both hands to dangle the sheet out in front of your body, holding it by its top edge. Shake it back and forth rapidly to set up a wave action which will be accompanied by an exciting rumbling sound—great for a sudden thunderstorm or the approach of a dreaded monster. (Sheet metal can be obtained at most large lumber supply stores. Inquire about a flat fiberglass panel at a large greenhouse supply center.) *Safety Note: Sheet metal provides the most satisfying rumble, but it does have thin edges which can possibly cut someone if handled carelessly.*

- This suggestion probably draws on your childhood experiences: Blow up a balloon, but don't knot it. Stretch its neck opening into a wide, thin shape and allow the air to escape slowly. The thin, nagging whine this produces could be the high-pitched buzz of a flying insect, the singing of a teakettle or the screeching chant of a witch.

- Run a stick along the side of an old-fashioned radiator, the exposed ridges of a sheet of corrugated cardboard or an old washboard.

- Slap the flat side of a book onto a table to produce the sound of a slamming door.

- Hit a section of metal pipe or a wood-splitting wedge with a hammer when you need a ringing blow of a miner's pick.

- The noisy, crackling type of plastic bag can create the sounds of a fire or fiercely burning sun. Just scrunch it, pull at it and shake it about. Do the same with a sheet of cellophane.

- Pour a handful of dried peas or uncooked popcorn kernels into an aluminum pie plate and swirl the plate in a horizontal circular motion. This creates an effective rattling roar evocative of heavy rain or waves breaking on a beach.

- Hum, warble or yodel through one end of a section of flexible vacuum cleaner hose. Now try making the same sounds as you whirl the other end of the hose around in a circle above your head.

- To simulate the clip-clop of horse hooves, try two coconut halves, plastic cups or plastic yogurt containers. Hold one in each hand and knock the open ends together.

SOUND EFFECTS THAT CAN BE PURCHASED

- Plastic flutes, recorders and different types of whistles can offer quite a range of sounds and provide simple musical accompaniment to your production. A good bird warble can be produced by rapidly covering and uncovering one or more of the sound holes while blowing steadily.

- A device called a Zube Tube™ can be purchased at children's toy stores. It is basically a long cardboard tube with a spring inside which produces strange, otherworldly sounds when shaken. If you speak into one of its ends, your voice will reverberate to become that of a mighty ogre or ancient god.

- A flexible plastic whirling tube with ridges can also be found in some toy stores. If you hold onto one end of it and whirl the rest around in a circle above your head, you will hear an eerie, haunting sound.

- A kazoo is a friendly little device. Simply hum into it and you become an instant musician. It also makes a great sound effect for bees and other buzzing insects. Make your own kazoo using a cardboard tube and wax paper (See the *Buzzing Bee Puppet* in Chapter 2).

- A slide whistle can add a humorous element to your sound effects kit. It can also provide some interesting wind and gale sounds.

- A harmonica is easy to use and takes up little space in your sound effects kit.

- A wind chime can add a moment of magic to your dramatization.

EASILY CONSTRUCTED SOUND EFFECTS

- You can make a simple stringed instrument from an empty facial tissues box, two pencils and some rubber bands. Stretch several rubber bands over the box so that the rubber bands reach over the hole. Slide a pencil under the rubber bands at either end of the hole so that the rubber bands are held up off the box. Stroke across the rubber bands with a finger or small, thin piece of plastic. For a variation on this idea, stretch rubber bands of different sizes over an empty picture frame.

- Use short pieces of string to dangle any combination of the following objects from a clothes hanger: spoons, bells, large nails, metal tubes. Hold the hanger up with one hand as you hit the items with a spoon or stick. Try shaking the hanger so the dangling items clang against each other.

- Attach several bells to a stick, an embroidery hoop or a plastic lid with sections of pipe cleaner.

- Shakers can be easily made and played. Put dried beans or uncooked popcorn kernels inside an empty container, tape on the lid and shake. Use any of the following items to hold the beans: two empty metal cans firmly taped together with duct tape, two paper bowls or aluminum pie plates facing each other and attached around the edges, film or tennis ball cans with lids firmly taped on, metal adhesive-bandage boxes, small sturdy cardboard boxes, and cardboard or plastic tubes with the ends covered by thin cardboard and taped closed.

- Create a shaker-rain tube by pouring a large handful of dried beans into a yard-long piece of stiff plastic tube. Close off the ends with doubled aluminum foil and duct tape. Hold the tube out horizontally in front of you. Slowly and gradually tip the tube toward one end so the beans begin to slide toward it. As they slide they will make a sound resembling falling rain or retreating ocean surf. This tube can also be played like a shaker; hold it in a horizontal position for best results.

- Strike two solid rounded sticks together.

- Cut a dozen lengths of crepe paper streamers, each roughly 2' long. Glue one end of each ribbon to a cardboard tube or the edge of a paper plate. When the glue is dry, hold the plate or tube in one hand and move it rapidly through the air. The streamers will produce an interesting turbulent sound.

- Glue sandpaper, rough side out, to two wooden blocks, then rub them together for a husky rhythm.

Choosing Sound Effects

After you've gathered a variety of sound effects, you and the children can decide what sounds to use in your dramatization. This is an exciting process. Think of it as painting a picture with sounds. There is no right or wrong choice; it is purely a matter of personal preference.

There are several ways to go about this, but the following is one approach that works well. Have children sit together on the floor or in chairs so they can all see and hear you. Pull out your sound effects bag and a copy of the story's narration. Explain that today's project will be choosing the sound effects for their show. Their job is to listen carefully so they can pick interesting sounds to help tell the story they will be enacting. Let them know that you will give them a chance to hear all the different sound effects before discussing how best to use them.

Hold up one of the sound effects, tell students its name, and give them a demonstration of the various sounds it can make—loud, soft, fast, slow, or any other combination or variation you can discover. Ask the children to think about the sounds as they hear them. Have them close their eyes and notice what pictures form in their heads as they listen. Is this a peaceful sound? An exciting sound? A sad sound? A scary sound? Can students think of a way to

get another kind of sound out of this object? Continue this demonstration until they have had a chance to hear many different possibilities. Give them an opportunity to offer suggestions.

Now it's time to choose sound effects for their story. Read through the story's narration, pausing whenever a sound effect seems in order, such as the entrance of a new character, an exciting action scene or a slow and graceful moment. Ask the children to suggest an appropriate sound or series of sounds that would help paint the picture their story is describing. You may want to give individual children an opportunity to choose a sound effect for their particular character. Choose the sound effects for more generalized action or interactions by the group through a vote of hands.

A pleasing effect is created by using the same little tune to begin and end a dramatization. This need not be anything fancy—a few simple notes played on the recorder or autoharp, a pattern of sounds made by tapping on the clothes hanger xylophone, a simple rhythm created on homemade drums, or a shake of a wind chime. If you or any of the children have any experience playing a musical instrument, a folk song representing the culture of the dramatized folktale could be played. Find a simple tune or musical phrase you feel comfortable with. You can, if you prefer, play a recording of a short piece of music.

Once all the sounds have been chosen and noted on the story's narrative script, ask the children to close their eyes and keep them closed. Read the story's narrative, pausing to add each chosen sound effect at its appointed place. When you have finished, ask the children if their sound effects helped them to "see" the story.

You may decide that a different method of choosing sound effects suits your group better. Consider the following options:

- Have the children be responsible for making or bringing in their own sound effects.

- Organize the children into two groups: performers and sound effects people. Give the sound effects people time to practice developing and performing their sounds for the story, just as the performers are given time to develop their puppets and masks and rehearse their character roles. After the story has been dramatized with its sound effects, the two groups could trade jobs for a new and different storytelling dramatization.

- If the story's narrator is also responsible for performing all of the sound effects, let the children choose their sound effects from a collection limited to those that the narrator would feel comfortable with. This will assure that the narrator will feel con-

fident to produce whatever sound effects the group decides on.

- If time is short and resources are scarce, vocal sound effects can be contributed by the audience. Have the narrator make a clearly lettered sign saying "**SOUND EFFECTS.**" Just before the storytelling dramatization begins, the narrator can inform the audience that it would be greatly appreciated if they would listen to the story and provide appropriate vocal sound effects whenever the sign appears. Then the narrator and the performers can begin acting out the story. The narrator can pause and hold up the sign whenever the story narration mentions a character or an event for which vocal sound effects would be desirable—the cheering of crowds, the swishing of a river, the whispering of leaves, the mooing of cows. The narrator should be prepared to prime the pump a little, if necessary, by producing a few vocal sound effects to give the audience the idea. This device directly involves the audience in the creative process of storytelling and makes the whole production a cooperative and memorable experience.

PERFORMING SOUND EFFECTS

If you want to add sound to your storytelling dramas, set up a sound effects table off to one side of the room. Make sure this location allows you a clear view of the performers in action—while staying out of their way. It is also important that the sound effects table does not block the audience's view of the performers. The table need not be invisible to the audience— the audience will enjoy seeing how sounds are produced—but you can place the table behind some type of screening if you prefer it to be out of sight.

Cover the table with a thick cloth or large towel to help keep the sound effects from rolling around or clanking together during the quiet parts of the story. Lay your chosen sound effects out on the table so they can be clearly seen and easily reached.

Write out a cue sheet to remind you which sounds go with which actions. Place this quick reference on the table where it can be scanned easily. If you are the narrator as well as the sound effects person, these sound cues can be written on your narrative script in a different color ink. Narrate the story from your position at the sound effects table.

If you are narrating the story and some of the children are responsible for the sound effects, you may still want to give your narration from a location close to the sound effects table so that you can give them assistance or guidance if needed.

Sound effects can be added effectively during pauses in the story's narration—places where the narrator would naturally stop to allow the performers time to enter, interact or complete an action. Used in this way, sound effects provide embellishment and punctuation to the dramatic interpretations of the performers.

Part Four

OPENING NIGHT

NINE

On with the Show

I Finished My Aardvark—Now What?

Folktales offer a wide variety of dramatic storytelling possibilities and provide an excellent opportunity to explore the traditional values, customs, art and costumes of other cultures. These stories evolve with each telling, and you can usually find several versions of the same story. Feel free to follow this tradition by shaping a folktale to fit the purposes of your dramatization.

In this chapter you will find all the information you will need to dramatize three international folktales. Once you have sharpened your skills with these guided tours, there will be no end to possibilities for future storytelling arts projects. Using puppets, masks and animated scenery, you can dramatize other folk and fairy tales, as well as original stories created by your students.

Each folktale presented here is in the narrative form. Ideas for dramatic action and sound effects can be found in parentheses. At the conclusion of each story, you will find a list of suggested puppets, masks, scenery and stages. Don't hesitate to make substitutions and improvements. Encourage children to contribute their own ideas about movements and sound effects. The storytelling arts offer a gratifying learning experience to everyone involved—enjoy the process.

General Advice

Read the story, minus stage directions, to the children to familiarize them with the characters before they begin the construction phase of the project.

As a general rule, the child who creates a puppet, mask or piece of moveable scenery should be the one to use it during the performance. Group scenery and prop projects are the exceptions, as these are constructed by many children and serve as scenery for the entire group.

Once your curtain is set up and the performance area is ready, it's a good idea to assign a waiting area to each group of performers. This is a place, usually offstage or behind the curtain, where the children wait until it is time for them to contribute to the action of the story. During the rehearsal you can designate a waiting area for each group. Remind students that rehearsals offer them a chance to practice waiting quietly. If there is a babble of background noise during the performance, it will be difficult for the audience to follow the story and for the performers to hear their cues.

When you and the children are setting up to rehearse, you may find that excitement runs high—as does the noise level. If you are trying to get everyone's attention focused on what you are about to say, it helps if you can provide an ear-catching signal to create an eddy of quiet—the boom of a drum or the ringing chime of a bell is usually effective and can save your vocal cords tremendous wear and tear. (A gong can be the perfect ear-catch-ing instrument as well as a wonderful sound effect for Asian stories.)

When rehearsing your storytelling dramatization, remind the children to listen to the narrator for their cues. The narrator slowly reads the story in a loud, clear voice, pausing to allow the performers time to perform dramatic action before continuing the story. When the narrator resumes speaking, it is usually a signal for the performers to wait quietly until their next scene of action.

The audience will have an easier time following the action of the story if the children understand the importance of waiting quietly, holding their puppets and scenery still until it is time for their characters to speak or perform. The eye is drawn to movement. If everyone is moving at once, it is difficult for the audience to decide where they should be looking.

You may find that there are more children in your group than the story can handle, or that some of the children missed out on the puppet and mask construction due to illness. These children can contribute to the group effort by helping to perform the sound effects or filling in for any absent performers.

If you are working with a very small group of children, each child can play more than one role in the story.

If you are working with a large group and performance space is tight, assign performance positions to the different groups so performers do not block each other from the audience's view.

If you are working with older children, give them the opportunity to use the more sophisticated techniques of papier-mâché sculpting or paper folding and engineering to create the features for their puppets and masks. When performing in front of the curtain, these puppeteers and scenery animators could wear plain dark clothing and black hoods to give them lower visibility.

It's a good idea for the narrator to practice reading the story out loud until he or she gains the confidence of familiarity. Experiment with verbal emphasis and pacing until you find the combination that sounds best to you.

Don't rehearse until you drop in an attempt to make the performance perfect. This is a learning experience for you and the children. Keep your sense of humor and stay flexible. Don't be afraid to improvise when the situation calls for it. A performance mistake or a prop failure can add a new dramatic element to the story; it could become the audience's favorite memory. During one kindergarten class's performance, the curtain fell over to reveal the puppeteers in various positions and stages of preparation. The following year the other classes were still talking about "that great story where the curtain fell over and you could see what was going on backstage."

Why Fish Can't Sing   *A Finnish Folk Tale*

This project features small puppets, a musical wizard called Väinämöinen (VY-na-moi'-nen), interactive scenery and several masked performers. Although this story is Finnish, it celebrates international diversity. It could accommodate thirteen to sixty children. This project can also be adjusted for a smaller group (See "Variations").

This group is using the Table Stage to perform *Why Fish Can't Sing*. Because the group pictured is small, it is using the adaptations suggested at the end of the performance guidelines (See "Variations").

STORY NARRATIVE

(Intro)

The story we would like to tell today is from a Scandinavian country with deep wild forests and many rivers, marshes and lakes. We call this country Finland. The Finns know it as *Suomi* (SWO-mee). People in Finland saw the Milky Way and called it the Path of Birds. Their stories reflect this poetic appreciation for the plants and animals of their world. This land of 200,000 lakes is home to many fish—an important food source for the people who first settled there—so fish play a role in their folktales. We would like to present *Why Fish Can't Sing*.

(Action: This is a good place to play a short and simple bit of music.)

The world was once a quiet place where beauty shone but no one spoke and all was silence. When spring's warm breath uncovered the moss, animals capered and peered about—but they did not bellow or bark.

(Animal Mouth Puppets are held up to silently hop, sway or gaze at each other for a minute or two. Then they disappear from view.)

Birds swooped and whirled through the air, but the sky did not ripple with their songs.

(Bird-in-the-Hand Puppets flap silently back and forth for a moment, then drop out of sight.)

The river waters danced round rocks and roots...

(Flowing River comes out from behind the curtain, swaying silently in serpentine curves, crosses in front of the curtain, then returns to wait behind it. If you are working with a small group of children, two of the animal puppeteers can hold a 2' or 3' strip of blue cloth above the curtain and wiggle it to imitate flowing water.)

and the cool winds blew across the marsh...

(Children in Wind Masks come out blowing *quietly* through their tubes—they should blow enough to make the tissue paper strips dance about but they should produce no noise. The children stand briefly in front of the curtain, their masks facing the audience, before returning backstage.)

but there was no splash—no sigh—no sound.
The people of the world had neither language nor laughter.

(Person Mouth Puppets are held above the curtain as far apart as possible. The puppets see each other and gather together. They stop and look at each other and at the audience as they stand around silently for a short time, then they sink out of sight.)

Then steadfast old Väinämöinen, that master of song and wizard of music, strode into view. He was stroking a *Kantele* (CAN teh leh)—his five-stringed harp with magical charms.

(The child in the Väinämöinen Paper Plate Mask enters slowly, majestically stroking the harp. Väinämöinen remains standing in view near one end of the curtain.)

All the creatures of the earth gathered around to listen. His music enchanted all who heard it.

(Animal, bird and people puppets poke up above the curtain and watch Väinämöinen)

"Ho ho! Why listen when you can sing along?" Väinämöinen said. "Choose the sound which you like best."

(Väinämöinen makes wide, sweeping gestures during this speech. The narrator can speak Väinämöinen's lines in a booming voice or try saying them through a Zube Tube™, or a whirling tube or a section of vacuum cleaner hose.)

Thunder liked the rolling rumble made by Väinämöinen's booming laughter.

(Children with Tumultuous Thunderclouds come out shaking their thunder sheets and stand in a group off to one side of the room. If the narrator has a section of flat sheet metal, this can be shaken to add to the rumblings.)

The wind preferred the gusty bellows of Väinämöinen's breath as he danced to his music.

(Children in Wind Masks come out blowing vigorously through their tubes and stand in a group on the other side of the room. The narrator can blow though a slide whistle or take long breaths in and out on the low notes of a harmonica.)

The bushy-top pines, the red-coned firs and the leafy birch felt that the murmuring rustle of Väinämöinen's clothing as he walked through the river reeds was the perfect speech for trees.

(Before the show starts, tape Shimmering Tree(s) to a chair(s) which is set in a spot where the audience can see it but where it will not block their view of the performers. Appoint a child to shake the tree(s) at this point in the story; a fish puppeteer would be a likely choice. The tree's sound effects can be supplemented by rustling a noisy plastic bag.)

The birds were inspired by the singing strings of Väinämöinen's harp. From these magical tones, the thrushes and larks, the ducks and the loons, and all the other birds were able to choose their songs.

(Bird-in-the-Hand Puppets flap back and forth, while the children who operate the puppets provide a vocal concert of bird calls. After a few moments of warbling flight, the birds disappear. A few trilling notes on a recorder or a warbling bird whistle adds a nice audio effect.)

The animals of the forest, field and marsh had listened carefully to Väinämöinen. With great excitement, they began to chatter and chirp, to clatter and croak.

(Animal Mouth Puppets rise above the curtain and open and close their mouths enthusiastically as they practice their calls. Each puppeteer repeats his or her animal cry several times, contributing to a raucous chorus of animal calls. When the narrator resumes speaking, the animals drop out of view.)

People from all over the earth studied the different sounds made by the magical Väinämöinen. They listened as he moved this way or that, and they heard the vibrating tones of his harp. They used all these sounds to create the many different languages of the world.

(The Person Mouth Puppets rise into view above the curtain. They open and close their mouths as the puppeteers enthusiastically call out words and phases in various languages. When the narrator begins speaking they drop out of sight.)

The river admired the swish and splash of his birch-bark shoes as he tromped across the marsh.

(The Flowing River winds out and stands swaying a little distance in front of the curtain as all the children in the cast, especially the river handlers, make swishing vocal sounds. The river remains in this position until the end of the story.)

Väinämöinen was delighted when he saw what was happening. "Your music pleases me. Continue!"

(Väinämöinen looks around and gestures during this speech. After the word "Continue" everyone—except for the fish—appears and repeats his or her characteristic sound at the same time, creating a cacophony of sounds. The river should be standing where the audience can see it clearly. When the narrator begins to speak again, everyone should stand quietly. It is very helpful if the narrator can use a single loud signal to let the children know it is time to stop their calls and sounds. A single booming beat of a drum works well, as does a clash of a cymbal or a pair of pot lids.)

Now while everyone else had been practicing their new sound and songs, the fish were quite another story. There they were—the salmon, the perch and the pike—swimming quietly beneath the waves.

(Fish puppeteers walk out making swimming motions with their Contemplative Fish puppets, which they are holding out in front of them—decorated side toward the audience. They "swim" their fish to a spot behind the river.)

They began to realize that something unusual was happening.

(The fish swim excitedly back and forth behind the river.)

Finally curiosity overcame them, and they timidly poked their heads out of the water to take a closer look.

(Fish puppets stand on their tails and poke their heads above the top edge of the river.

They didn't show much of themselves—only enough to see what was going on. They saw the mouths of all the other creatures opening and closing. But the ears of the fish were still underwater, so they could not hear any of the sounds the others were making.

(All puppets with movable mouths open and close their mouths silently at this point.)

Nevertheless, they did not want to be left out. They decided to act just like the others. Slowly the mouths of the fish began to open and close…

(Fish puppeteers move control rods to make the fish mouths open and close.)

but they did not make a sound.

Even to this day, if you watch the fish, you will see them opening and closing their mouths, but you will not hear a single song come out of them.

(Repeat introductory musical theme, if you used one.)

And that is the end of our story.
Hyvästi
(HEW-vas-teh' means "good-bye" in Finnish.)

(Everyone moves to the front of the curtain and bows to the audience.)

PUPPETS, MASKS, SCENERY

Characters	What to Construct	Number
people of the world	Person Mouth Puppets	3 to 10
animals of the world	Animal Mouth Puppets	3 to 10
river	1 Flowing River*	0 to 3 children
fish	Contemplative Fish Puppets	2 to 4
wind	Wind Masks	1 to 10
thunder	Tumultuous Thundercloud Scenery	1 to 12
birds	Bird-in-the-Hand Puppets	2 to 10
Väinämöinen	Paper Plate Mask	1

*You only need one river but its construction and manipulation can require from 0 to 3 children depending on your needs. (See "Additional Props and Information" section that follows.)

Stage

If you are working with a small group of twenty children or less, the simple Table Stage works well for this dramatization. If you have twenty to sixty children in your group, you may want to line up two or more long tables for an extended version of the Table Stage. You could also use any of the other stages described in this book. The children can decorate the curtain as a group scenery project.

Group Scenery Projects

1. Children could decorate the stage curtain with their versions of Finnish scenery. Finland is a land of many lakes, marshes and deep forests of pine, spruce, fir and birch trees. It has numerous streams and rivers which form rapids as they flow to the sea. It has mountains in the north. Wooden houses are common because lumber is plentiful.

2. Make one or more Shimmering Trees to represent Finland's dense forests.

Additional Props and Information

• For the purposes of this story, children can make their Animal Mouth Puppets into any creatures they wish, as long as the animals have recognizable calls. (Rabbits, earthworms and giraffes need not apply.) Squirrels, moose, wolves, elks, bears, foxes, weasels, cows, sheep, horses, lynxes, goats, pigs, dogs, cats, mice, snakes, frogs, and toads are some of the animals found in Finnish folktales.

• The Bird-in-the-Hand Puppets should also have a call or song. The sparrow, titmouse, swallow, woodpecker, chickadee, wren, crow, raven, wood grouse, eagle, loon, sea gull, chicken, duck, and goose are among the birds mentioned in Finnish folklore.

• The children who are making Contemplative Fish Puppets can decorate them in any style they like. Whitefish, pike, salmon and perch are some of the fish found in Finland's waters.

• If you are working with a large group of children, the Flowing River (See "Scenery in Motion," Chapter 6) can be constructed and operated by two or three children. The fish can use the Flowing River as a portable curtain. If you are working with a small group, drape a blue scarf over the top central part of the stage curtain to represent the river. Someone can give it an animating shake when it learns to speak, and the Contemplative Fish can poke their heads up from behind the stage curtain in the area behind the blue scarf.

• Finnish lore describes Väinämöinen as having a long white beard, so provide this child with plenty of white crepe paper streamers in addition to the other suggested mask making materials. This child will also need to construct a simple five-stringed instrument to represent Väinämöinen's kantele. (See "Easily Constructed Sound Effects" in Chapter 8.)

• The Person Mouth Puppets are supposed to represent all the people in the world, so encourage variety. Display pictures of people in traditional costumes from several different countries. Ask the entire group of children to contribute any greetings or phrases they know from different languages. The Person Mouth Puppets can repeat these phrases when they are speaking all the languages of the world. If the children do not know any words from another language, they could learn some of the following greetings. (It would be a nice touch if a few of the people puppeteers learned the Finnish and Swedish greetings, as those are the two official languages of Finland.)

päivää
Finnish: pronounced PIE-vaa

hej hej
Swedish: hay-hay

ohayo
Japanese: oh-HI-oh

buon giorno
Italian: BWOHN-JOR-noh

aloha
Hawaiian: ah-LOH-hah

hola
Spanish: OH-la

guten morgan
German: GOO-ten MORE-gun

bon jour
French: bone ZHUR

salaam
Arabic: sah-LAHM

Positioning

The Shimmering Tree or Trees can be placed in front of the curtain, near an end.

The Person Mouth and Animal Mouth Puppets can wait behind the curtain until it is time for them to appear above it.

The Bird-in-the-Hand Puppets can be held up from behind the curtain to fly along its top, or the puppeteers can fly their birds out and across the front of the curtain before returning to their waiting spot. The children who operate these puppets should be assigned waiting places behind the curtain. (If your backstage area is congested, the birds can join the performers who wait off to the side of the room—they can fly their puppets across the room to the front of the curtain when it is time for them to make their appearance.)

Tumultuous Thundercloud and Wind Mask performers can wait off to the sides of the room, walking over to stand in front of the curtain when it is time for them to perform their actions.

If you are using the Flowing River active scenery cloth, the two or three children who are operating it can wait off to the side of the room until it is time for them to wind their way to the performance area in front of the curtain.

The Contemplative Fish should wait off to the side of the room with the Flowing River. They swim out to a spot behind the portable river and poke their heads above it when the story suggests this action. If you are work-ing with a small group of children, the fish can wait behind the area of the stage curtain which is draped with the blue scarf, from which they pop up at the appropriate time.

Väinämöinen can wait behind the stage curtain or off to one side of the room. Once he makes an appearance, he can remain standing near one end of the curtain and facing the audience.

Variations

• If you are working with a small group of children or have a small performance space, make a single small thundercloud from a piece of poster board and attach it to a control rod. This cloud can be held up from behind the curtain to represent thunder.

Also, glue several 2' crepe paper streamers to a cardboard tube to represent the wind. A child can hold this above the curtain, moving it slowly back and forth so the streamers dance in the air currents.

• If space is not a problem, you might want to substitute the High-Flying Birds for the smaller Bird-in-the-Hand Puppets. These large rod puppets can wait off to the side, then flap slowly back and forth in front of the curtain when it is time to make their appearance.

The Ogre's Staircase *A Japanese Folktale*

Singing Stars

Drifting Moon

Hand/Mouth Villager puppet

Overbearing Ogre puppet

Ladder Curtain Stage

Darkness masks

Black poster board footprints

Poster Board Garden with vegetables

Enchanting Fairy puppet

Boisterous Chicken puppets

This group is performing *The Ogre's Staircase*, complete with a three-rod Overbearing Ogre Puppet in all its glory.

This project revolves around a large three-person rod puppet. The cast includes smaller rod puppets, marionettes, masks, and Hand-Mouth Puppets. It can be dramatized by a group of children numbering anywhere from nine to fifty-five.

If you want to dramatize this story with children as young as five and six years of age, ask an adult or older child to help the younger children support the ogre's main control rods, scale down the size of the ogre puppet, or replace the ogre puppet with a child wearing a Grocery Bag Mask depicting an ogre.

A pronunciation guide to the Japanese words spoken by the narrator can be found in "Additional Props and Information" which follows the story.

STORY NARRATIVE

(Intro)

The story we would like to tell today is from Japan, a country of mountainous islands known as the Land of the Rising Sun. The rising sun and the rooster who heralds it are important elements in this story. The Japanese people revere the beauty of their land. And—like people everywhere—they appreciate a good story. We would like to present our version of a Japanese folktale called The Ogre's Staircase.

(Action: Optional musical theme)

**Long, long ago there was a towering mountain.
At the foot of this mountain was a little farming village.**

(Narrator gestures toward the curtain decorated with mountain and village scenery.)

On the other side of the mountain lived a terrible ogre.

(Overbearing Ogre Puppet is raised up behind curtain so the ogre's head glares out at the audience over the top edge of the curtain. After a few moments, he sinks back down and out of sight. The ogre's appearance should be accompanied by a loud and dynamic sound effect. Try beating a cymbal or a drum, or shaking a large Zube Tube™ or thunder sheet.)

One morning as the sun rose over the mountain...

(The Flamboyant Sun rises slowly from behind curtain until it hovers above the top edge of the curtain. Accompany the sun's rise with whatever sound effect seems right to you: shaker, crinkling plastic bags, wood block, gong or a rising scale played on a xylophone.)

its appearance was greeted by the enthusiastic crowing of the village rooster.

(The Boisterous Chicken Puppet stretches its head into the air as the child operating the rooster crows loudly. The other Boisterous Chicken Puppets begin to cluck and move about the floor.)

The villagers awoke, had a breakfast of fish and rice and began their daily chores.

(The children operating the Hand-Mouth villager puppets come out from behind the curtain and stand in front of it. They hold their puppets out in front of their chests and faces. The puppets stretch and yawn and greet each other. *Ohayo*—pronounced like the state of Ohio—is a Japanese greeting.)

They fed their chickens...

(The villager puppets scatter imaginary grain to the chickens. The villager puppeteers can call out "sah, sah" [come, come] as their puppets scatter torn paper pieces on the floor near the chickens. The chickens cluck at the villagers and peck eagerly at the "grain" on the floor.)

and they began to weed the community vegetable garden.

(The villager puppets proceed to the garden and reach down making weeding gestures.)

They soon noticed that some of their vegetables had been trampled.

(Villager puppets point at the garden, mumble to each other and throw their hands into the air in gestures of surprise.)

On closer examination, they saw that the footprints which crossed their garden could only be those of the mountain *oni*—a terrible ogre.

(One or two of the villager puppets pick up the big poster board footprints and hold them high in the air for the audience to see. The other villagers point excitedly at the footprints.)

"Yare! Yare!" **they shouted. "The terrible oni has done this wicked thing!"**

(Villager puppets make fists and wave them at the mountain.)

Goro! Goro! **the very ground rumbled as the oni approached them.**

(The ogre puppet comes out in front of the curtain and stops in a location where he is to one side of the villagers and facing the audience. Repeat the ogre's sound effect until he stops. Cymbal crescendos, a large drum or a Zube Tube™ would be a good sound effect for the ogre.)

He was a towering giant with skin as green as cat's eyes, a mouth like a great black cavern, and two sharp horns protruding from his head.

"You must give me a child every day for my supper, or else I will destroy all your crops," said the oni. His voice sounded like boulders rolling down a mountain canyon.

(The ogre should gesture with his arms as the narrator says his lines. The ogre's lines can be spoken into a Zube Tube™ or through a whirling tube for greater effect.)

"A child for your supper? Why should we give you our children?" cried the angry villagers.

(Make sure the villagers understand that they should be turned toward the audience so their puppets can be seen. They can turn their puppet's heads so they appear to be looking at the ogre, and they can wave their fists and wag their fingers at the ogre, but the children should try to avoid turning their backs to the audience.)

"Because I am more powerful than all of you puny farmers put together—Ha, Ha, Ha!" His boastful voice echoed around the mountain.

(The children who operate the Flamboyant Sun, Drifting Moon, and Singing Stars can provide the echo by calling out "Ha, ha, haaaaaa!" from behind the curtain.)

The villagers knew that mountain ogres, though terrifying, are lazy dim-witted creatures. They decided to challenge the oni in order to gain more time.

"If you can hack a stone stairway to the top of the mountain in a single night, you will prove your great strength and we will have to do what you say."

(The villager Hand-Mouth Puppets gesture toward the curtain.)

"I'll finish it before that cock crows, or I'll leave this mountain forever," bragged the ogre.

(The ogre points at the rooster and then boastfully at his own chest.)

The sun began to sink behind the mountain.

(The Flamboyant Sun sinks slowly behind curtain. Provide the sun's sound effect. If you are using a xylophone, play a descending scale.)

The villagers returned to their homes. They spread their quilts on top of their *tatami*, and fell into a fitful sleep as darkness fell.

(The villagers walk back behind the curtain. If you have a group of children wearing Paper Plate Masks to represent darkness, they can come out when the villagers are behind the curtain. They crisscross in front of the curtain a couple of times—facing the audience—with their masks held in front of their faces and their streamers flowing. The whirling tube is a good sound effect for darkness, or you could rub two sandpaper blocks together, blow across the top of a bottle, or choose some other sound which seems to fit the scene.)

The stars shimmered into view.

(The Singing Stars pop up above the curtain and vibrate to provide a soft, ringing sound effect. If your group is small and you decided not to have stars, just skip any reference to them.)

The moon came out bright and clear.

(The Drifting Moon rises up from behind the curtain. Provide a sound effect to accompany this. A few simple drawn-out notes on a flute or recorder would do.)

When the villagers were asleep, the oni draped a piece of cloth over the rooster's head.

(The ogre walks over to the rooster puppet and lowers the hand with the cloth. The child operating the rooster unclips the cloth and drapes it over the rooster's head. The rooster should then be held up to show the audience its cloth-covered head.)

"Now the rooster cannot see the sunrise, so he will not crow. The villagers will oversleep and I'll have plenty of time to finish carving the staircase.
Gishi gashi, gishi gashi," the oni huffed and puffed as he lifted his heavy pick into the air and began to hack stone stairs into the side of the mountain.

(The ogre walks over to face the center front of the curtain. He raises his pick hand slowly far above his head and brings it down in a great slow sweep toward the curtain—stopping just short of actual contact. He repeats this movement several times. Every time the ogre's pick appears to hit the curtain, a percussive sound effect should be provided. Try hitting a metal pipe with a hammer, or give a ringing blow to a cymbal.)

Luckily, some fairies lived in a nearby forest. These wood sprites saw the mean trick the oni had played on the villagers. They knew the villagers to be dutiful and hard working, and they decided to help them.

(The Enchanting Fairy marionettes float out slowly and gracefully from their forest. The children should hold their marionettes up and out in front of their bodies so the audience can see them. If you have only one fairy, adjust the narrative to the singular. A wind chime makes a nice musical sound effect for fairies.)

Sawa sawa, their robes rustled softly as they approached the rooster. They danced round and round him until the breezes created by their swirling garments blew the cloth from the rooster's head.

(The fairies float slowly out of their forest and begin a slow dance around the rooster, circling him several times. After the child operating the rooster puppet removes the cloth from the rooster's head, the fairies return to the forest.)

Before the oni had finished the staircase, the sun began to rise above the mountain's peak.

(The moon and stars disappear and the sun rises into view from behind the curtain. Provide the sun's sound effect.)

The rooster crowed vigorously.

(The rooster lifts his head and crows loudly. The rest of the chickens cluck and begin to move around.)

The villagers awoke and saw that the oni's stairway was not yet finished. "*Oya! Oya!* We are saved," they shouted.

(The villager puppets come out and gesture toward the mountain, then look toward the ogre. They should have their pipe cleaner picks with them this time.)

"I have lost" cried the oni.
He shook his head sadly and walked away.

(The ogre shakes his head slowly, then droops his head and shoulders and walks slowly behind the curtain. Provide the ogre's sound effect as he walks away, but keep it subdued.)

That oni was never seen again.
The villagers finished the staircase.

(The villagers walk over to the central front part of the curtain and make motions with their picks as if they are hacking a staircase into the mountain. To simulate the sound of their pick work, hit the bottom of an empty metal can with a chopstick or pencil. Better yet, arrange for several children to tap on metal cans. The children who play the part of the chicken, stars, or darkness could help with this sound effect. As the villagers swing their picks, one of the villager puppeteers should be responsible for pressing the sections of sheet between the ladder steps against pieces of sticky doubled-over duct tape on each step. When the villagers have finished with their picks, it will look as if they have really carved a stairway into the mountain.)

On special clear summer evenings, they would climb the staircase into the fresh, cool mountain air, just as the sun was setting.

(As the sun sinks slowly, the sun's sound effect should be heard and the villager puppets should be climbing up the stairway. As the puppets reach the top of the curtain stairway, they should turn off to either side and move along the top edge of the curtain, out to the ends of the curtain pole. When the puppets reach the end of the curtain, puppeteers can step behind the curtain—while continuing to hold their puppets on top, facing out toward the audience. When all the puppeteers are standing behind the curtain, they should spread out so that the puppets are distributed along the top edge of the curtain.)

There they would watch darkness spread over the neat green fields far below,

(The children in darkness masks swirl into view and crisscross in front of the curtain a few times. Provide the sound effect for darkness.)

The stars would wink into view…

(Stars pop up into sight from behind the curtain and ring their bells.)

and share in the viewing of the full moon as it floated slowly and gracefully over the mountain.

(The moon rises slowly from behind the curtain. Its appearance should be accompanied by its sound effect. The villagers point at the moon. They can also make verbal sounds of appreciation—"oohs" and "aahs". This would be a good place to repeat the optional musical theme.)

And so we reach the end of our story.
Sayonara.

(Sayonara means "good-bye" in Japanese.) Everybody comes out in front of the curtain holding their puppets, masks and portable scenery. All bow to the audience.

PUPPETS, MASKS, SCENERY

Characters	What to Construct	Number
chickens (1 rooster plus hens)	Boisterous ChickenPuppets	2 to 10
fairy (fairies)	Enchanting Fairy Marionettes	1 to 10
darkness (optional)	Paper Plate Masks	0 to 10
villagers	Hand-Mouth Puppets	2 to 10
ogre	1 Overbearing Ogre Puppet	3 children
sun and moon	Flamboyant Sun and Drifting Moon Scenery	1 to 2
stars (optional)	Singing Star Scenery	0 to 10

Stage

The Ladder Curtain Stage is ideal for this story, because the stepladder's steps can serve as the mountain stairway. To prepare for the dramatization, fold pieces of duck tape into double-stick circles (See "Masking Tape" in "What Materials to Use," Chapter 1). Press one or two pieces of this double-stick tape to the top surface of each step of the stepladder. When the sheet is pressed against these pieces of tape during the dramatization, the curtain will take on the form of a stairway.

If you prefer to use a different type of stage, you could ask the children to draw an ascending stairway on a long strip of cloth. Attach this stairway securely its top edge to the top center area of the stage curtain. It can be flipped back behind the curtain until the narration calls for the stairway to be completed. Then flip the cloth stairway forward and over the curtain support so it will hang down in front of the curtain.

Group Scenery Projects

1. Decorate the stage curtain. Use oil pastels, felt-tip markers or tempera paints to decorate a white sheet with mountain plants and scenery. Japanese village houses can be cut out of construction paper, then attached to the bottom part of the curtain with rolled double-stick masking tape. Japanese mountains have forests of maple, ash, birch, beech, poplar, bamboo, fir, spruce, pine, and Japanese cedar. Cherry trees bloom along the riverbanks. Traditional houses were once made of paper and wood so they could be rebuilt easily after earthquakes and fires. Farmhouses in rural villages often had thatched roofs. Lower mountain slopes might have terraced rice paddies.

2. Make vegetables out of construction paper or poster board for the village garden. (Directions for the Poster Board Garden can be found in Chapter 6.) Cabbages, onions, carrots, sweet potatoes, burdock root, and sugar beets are some of the vegetables grown in rural Japan.

3. Make leaves out of metallic paper and tape them to small branches attached to chairs (See the Shimmering Tree in Chapter 6). Several of these branches could form the forest where the wood fairies live.

Additional Props and Information

• Japanese words are usually pronounced with equal stress on each syllable. There are many uses of onomatopoeia (words whose sounds suggest their meaning) in Japanese folktales; you will find several in this story:

goro goro (rumbling):
pronounced goh-roh goh-roh.

sawa sawa (rustling noise):
sah-wah sah-wah.

gishi gashi (huffing and puffing):
geeh-shee gah-shee.

oya oya (a cheer):
oh-yah oh-yah.

yare yare (Oh me! Oh no!):
yah-rei, yah-rei.

sah sah (come come):
sah-sah.

oni (ogre):
oh-nee.

tatami (woven rush mat):
tah-tah-mee.

sayonara (good-bye):
sah-yo-nah-rah.

• Designate one of the Boisterous Chicken Puppets as the rooster. Decorate its head with a large, erect comb and its rear with an imposing and ostentatious tail.

• If your performance has only one fairy, adjust the narrative to fit the cast.

• Darkness masks are Paper Plate Masks on a stick. The children darken the masks with abstract designs in dark purple, blue and black colors, and glue several 2' black crepe paper streamers around the edges of the plates. When performing, the children can hold the masks in front of their faces, moving them up and down or swirling them in a circular motion to make the crepe paper ribbons dance.

• When the children are making the villager Hand-Mouth Puppets, provide them with black construction paper to form the hair. Lightweight artificial flowers and crepe paper streamer headbands are also useful options for developing the characters. Try to display pictures of Japanese people in tra-

ditional dress so children can refer to them as they work.

• Make sure that the child who is making the Drifting Moon understands that this story calls for a full moon.

• Each villager puppet will also need a pick, which the children can easily make. Give each child two pipe cleaners. Bend each pipe cleaner in half and twist the double strands together for strength. Twist the end of one doubled pipe cleaner around the middle of the second doubled pipe cleaner forming a little T-shape pick. The puppeteers can hold these in their gesturing hands when the villager puppets work on the staircase.

• Japanese ogres are often pictured with one or two horns. Tape cone-shape paper cups to the Overbearing Ogre's head if horns are desired.

Twisted pipe cleaners make simple picks for the villager puppets.

• To make the ogre's pick, tape two paper-towel size cardboard tubes together to form a T shape. Children can paint it while they are painting the ogre's head, or they can simply cover it with a coat of aluminum foil. When the pick is dry, place its handle in one of the ogre's hands, wrap the ogre's fingers around it and fasten it in place with staples or clear plastic tape.

• Tape a spring-type clothespin to the palm of the ogre's free hand. Make sure it still opens and closes easily after the tape job. Attach a lightweight handkerchief to the ogre's hand by means of

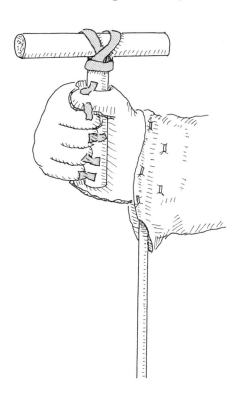

Construct the ogre's T-shape pick from two paper towel tubes and masking tape. Fasten it to the ogre's hand with clear plastic tape or staples.

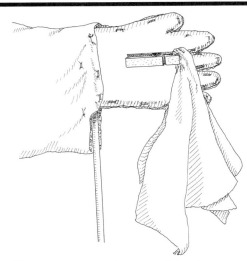

The ogre can carry the rooster's head covering by means of a spring-type clothespin.

the clothespin. The cloth will serve as the rooster's hood, which the ogre can carry in his hand until it is time to cover the rooster's head.

• Each of the children working on the ogre puppet should draw and cut out a big footprint from a sheet of black poster board. Encourage them to make the footprints as large as the poster board will allow; they can use white chalk to draw the footprint shapes. Lay these footprints on top of and around the vegetable garden before the dramatization of the story begins.

• If the children's ogre puppet does not conform to the story's description of the ogre, adjust the narration so it more closely describes their puppet.

Positioning

The children operating the stars, sun and moon can wait behind the curtain but should stay well back from it. When it is time for them to appear, they can approach the curtain and hold their props up behind it.

The villagers should also have a waiting place behind the curtain, but they should be prepared to step out in front of the curtain when it is time for the villager puppets to make an appearance. The pipe cleaner picks, which the villagers use later in the story, can be placed on the floor near their waiting place.

The ogre puppet, with a pick taped to one hand and a rooster-hooding cloth dangling from the clothespin on the other, should wait well behind the curtain or in another room with an adjoining doorway. He should come out in front of the curtain when it is time for him to talk to the villagers.

Set up the forest of Shimmering Trees off to the side of the room, and have the wood fairies wait there until it is time for them to approach the rooster. The fairy puppeteers can sit on the chairs to which the Shimmering Trees are attached.

The masked darkness performers can wait on the other side of the room, with their masks turned away from the audience, until it is time for them to enact the approach of darkness.

The chicken puppeteers can sit on the floor some distance in front of the curtain and in full view of the audience. Make sure the puppeteers do not block the audience's view of their puppets. The chickens should be held with their sides presented to the audience, as their front view is narrow and insubstantial.

Place the vegetable garden on the floor some distance in front of the curtain and slightly off to one side. Lay out the black poster board footprints on the floor around and across the vegetable garden.

Variations

• Use Quick-and-Easy Hand Puppets for the villager puppets.

• If you are working with a small group, dramatize the story without stars or darkness masks, or combine the roles with the same children playing both. The sun and moon can be combined into one prop, with the sun on one side and the moon on the other.

• If your time is short or your performance space small, have a child play the ogre by wearing a Grocery Bag Mask.

The Singing Drum   *An African Folktale*

Flamboyant Sun scenery

Stately Giraffe puppet

Paper Plate mask (Amanzi's parents)

Poster Board Rod puppet

Curtain

Hand/Mouth puppet (Amanzi)

Grocery Bag mask (Ogre)

Ocean cloth

Poster Board Animal mask with body cloth and poster board cylinder legs

This project features several large two-person animal puppets and plenty of parts for masked performers. It provides an enjoyable dramatic experience for seventeen to sixty-two children.

Young children can make masks from paper plates and bags. Older children can perform the story in more sophisticated papier-mâché masks.

STORY NARRATIVE

(Intro)

The story we are about to tell is from the *Xhosa* (KOH seh) people—one of the African Bantu tribes. When the Xhosa settled in southern Africa, they found security in their tribal villages, for they believed that the forest, brush, grassy plains, and other lonely spots were the homes of dangerous spirits. This story reflects those fears. It also demonstrates the Xhosan characteristic of being generous and hospitable toward visitors. We would like to tell you the story of *The Singing Drum*.

(Action: Optional musical theme. The children backstage create a soft background noise of animal and insect sounds.)

One morning a little girl named Amanzi went to the shore to look for shells. She planned to use these shells to decorate her father's hunting pouch.

(The child operating the Amanzi Hand-Mouth Puppet comes out from behind the curtain and stands alongside the ocean cloth. One of the puppeteer's hands should be operating the puppet's head and the other hand can be placed through Amanzi's sleeve to hold a paper bag bowl. The bowl can be placed on the ground near the ocean. As Amanzi searches the ground for shells and places them in her bag bowl, the puppet should face the audience as much as possible.)

As she placed the beautiful shells in her calabash bowl, she began to sing.

(The child operating the Amanzi puppet begins to sing a simple repetitive song while opening and closing the puppet's mouth.)

Amanzi loved to sing. She often made up her own songs. Her voice was so beautiful that all the animals and insects stopped to listen.

(The hum of background sounds suddenly stops.)

But they were not the only ones listening. Hidden in the brush nearby was a large man. He was wearing a string of leopard's teeth around his wrist, and he was carrying a drum.

(The child wearing the Grocery Bag Mask steps out from behind the opposite end of the curtain holding the drum and stands there watching the Amanzi puppet as she sings. Provide a foreboding sound effect when the ogre makes his appearance. Try a few sudden startling beats on a drum or the bottom of a large empty can, or the ominous hiss of one or two shakers.)

Although he looked like a large, well-fed man, he was really an ogre. He crept closer to Amanzi.

(The ogre tiptoes slowly over to stand next to the singing Amanzi puppet.)

Then he grabbed her by the back of her neck, and stuffed her into his big drum.

(The ogre sets his drum on the floor and opens its lid. Then he grabs the Amanzi puppet—carefully pulls it off the puppeteer's hand—and puts the puppet inside his drum. As the Amanzi puppet is being moved into the drum, Amanzi's puppeteer steps quietly behind the curtain.)

"What a wonderful voice," said the ogre. "You sound like a singing bird. Whenever I beat my drum, you must sing for me. The villagers will admire my magical drum and will feed me well. If you do not sing, I will eat you."

(The narrator can speak the ogre's lines in a loud, boastful voice. The ogre can shake a finger sternly at the drum while these lines are being spoken.)

As you can well imagine, Amanzi was very frightened and tried to think of a plan. She could call for help, but she knew she was too far away from her village for anyone to hear her. So she decided she would sing—but only her own songs. Maybe someone from her village would recognize her voice and help her escape.
    The ogre picked up his drum and walked away.

(The ogre picks up his drum and walks around in the area in front of the curtain.)

He traveled to a distant village.

(Children wearing villager Paper Plate Masks come out and stand in a group near the end of the curtain opposite the ocean. They should face the audience. The ogre approaches the villagers, stopping next to them.)

"Villagers, I am tired and hungry. If you let me spend the night in your village, I will play my magical singing drum for you."

(The ogre gestures while the narrator speaks.)

The villagers welcomed their visitor graciously, assuring him that they would love to hear his drum, if he was not too tired.

(The villagers gesture their welcome and invite the ogre to stay. They examine his drum with interest.)

"Now I will play my drum for you, and it will sing like a little bird," said the ogre.

(The ogre sets his drum down and stands behind it.)

He began to beat his drum.

(The ogre mimes beating the drum using big arm movements. The ogre should stop just short of actually hitting the drum. Provide appropriate sound effects by *softly* drumming on a drum, tin or the sound effects table with your hands.)

Amanzi began to sing.

(The child who made the Amanzi puppet sings Amanzi's song loudly from behind the curtain. The child should sing through a cardboard tube or a rolled-up newspaper so the song will sound as if it is coming from a hollow drum.)

The ogre played his drum until the moon glided into the enormous night sky.

(The Drifting Moon Scenery rises from behind the curtain, glides gracefully along above the curtain, then sinks slowly out of sight behind the curtain. Provide a sound effect for the moon. Jingling bells, playing a few notes on a recorder or blowing across the top of a plastic bottle are possibilities. If the children made Singing Stars, they can hold them up from behind the curtain when the moon appears and the following cue line can be added to the narrative: "and brilliant stars glowed like coals.")

"Now I must stop," said the ogre, "for I am very hungry."
    The villagers were grateful for the beautiful music. They offered their finest food to the ogre: fat pumpkins and sweet yams, ripe melons and thick porridge, golden bananas and foaming goat's milk, red beans and roasted meat.
    The ogre ate greedily.

(While the narrator is speaking, the villagers offer their containers of food to the ogre, who lifts various items of food into the air before appearing to stuff them into the mouth area of his mask. The ogre should stand facing the audience so they can easily see him as he makes gestures of cramming food into his mouth. Remind the villagers not to block the audience's view of the ogre as they offer him food.)

Finally, even the ogre could eat no more, and he began to stretch and yawn.

(The ogre makes stretching movements and covers his mask mouth with his hand.)

When the villagers saw he was tired, they politely bid him good night and returned to their huts to sleep.

(The villagers pick up the food and food baskets and move out of sight behind the curtain.)

When everyone had fallen asleep, the ogre opened his drum.
   "Here is your dinner, Amanzi," he said as he dropped five little beans into the drum. The selfish ogre had eaten everything else.

(After opening the drum, the ogre makes five large arm gestures as he pretends to drop the beans into the drum. A sound effect should be provided each time an imaginary bean is dropped into the drum. Hit a wood block or beat on the bottom of a metal can once for each bean.)

The ogre then closed his drum tightly and fell fast asleep.

(The ogre closes the drum, then lays down on the floor and pretends to sleep.)

In the morning, the hot African sun bleached the sky.

(The Flamboyant Sun Scenery rises from behind the curtain. Provide a sound effect for the sun. Try crinkling a sheet of cellophane, playing an ascending scale on a xylophone or whirl dried beans around in an aluminum pie plate. The sun is held up for a few moments as the action continues, then it disappears quietly behind the curtain.)

The ogre awoke… picked up his drum… and walked away looking for another village.

(The ogre performs these actions as the narrator pauses for each and disappears behind the curtain.)

When Amanzi did not return, her parents went to the seashore to search for her.

(The children in parent Paper Plate Masks come out in front of the curtain on the ocean side. They look around in all directions, holding one flat hand horizontally above the eyes in a classic searching gesture.)

They found her calabash filled with pretty shells but did not see Amanzi.

(Amanzi's mother lifts the paper bag bowl from the floor, shows it to Amanzi's father, then places it back on the floor.)

They began to search the brushy woods and grassy plains, when they met a giraffe taking dainty steps as it looked for tasty acacia leaves.

(The Stately Giraffe Puppet walks out. It stops to examine the tree scenery on the front of the curtain. Provide a sound effect for the giraffe's approach. A few climbing notes on a wind instrument or a slide whistle are possibilities.)

"Please help us, giraffe," called Amanzi's parents. "You can see over the treetops; can you see our daughter, Amanzi?"

(The parents approach the giraffe during this dialogue. They make pleading gestures with their hands.)

The giraffe stretched out its neck and looked out over the wide plains. When the giraffe turned back to Amanzi's parents, it only shook its head slowly before wandering away.

(The giraffe puppet lifts its head high and peers about. Then it turns toward Amanzi's parents, lowers its head slightly and shakes it slowly from side to side. It walks out of sight. Provide the giraffe's sound effect for its departure.)

Amanzi's parents continued their search. They walked on until they felt the ground begin to tremble.

(Provide a suitable sound effect. Several deep drumbeats, rumblings from a thunder sheet or a rising crescendo on a cymbal would work well. The parents react to the sound effects by trembling, holding onto each other and looking around anxiously.)

They saw an enormous elephant emerging from the tall grasses like a great gray ghost.

(The elephant approaches the parents accompanied by the continued sound effect. The elephant stops next to the parents. The sound effect stops.)

"Great elephant, with your wonderfully big ears, have you heard the sweet voice of our dear Amanzi?"

(The parents gesture while their lines are being spoken. The elephant cocks its head to the side as if listening.)

But the elephant's great ears flapped sadly as it shook its great head and slowly rumbled away.

(The elephant shakes its head as it walks slowly back to its waiting place. Repeat the elephant's sound effects until it is out of sight.)

Amanzi's parents did not give up hope. Suddenly they stopped, for they saw a tawny lion bounding through the grass.

(The Saw-Toothed Lion Puppet comes out and stops in front of the curtain next to Amanzi's parents and facing the audience. Provide an exciting sound effect to accompany the lion's entrance. You could make a few hard sharp hits on a woodblock, run a stick along a radiator or scrape a vegetable grater with a spoon.)

"Oh lion, with your sharp white teeth, you haven't eaten our little daughter, have you?"

(Parents make appropriate gestures while the narrator is speaking their lines. They might point to the lion's teeth, then cover their own mask mouths in horror.)

The lion shook its great shaggy mane. It had eaten a fat Zebra that morning and was ready for a nap. It yawned tiredly and bounded away to find a shady spot.

(The lion puppet shakes its head, opens its mouth in a big toothy yawn, then moves out of sight. Provide the lion's sound effect until it moves out of sight.)

Amanzi's parents traveled for many weeks searching for their little lost daughter.

(The parents wander back and forth making searching gestures.)

One night, tired and dusty, they arrived at a village.

(The parents walk slowly with sagging shoulders. The villagers come out in front of the curtain and gather near one end, facing the audience.)

"Bota," said the villagers, greeting them graciously. "You look very tired. You are welcome to spend the night in our village."

(The villagers make welcoming gestures.)

There was another guest in the village that night. It was a man with a drum.

(The ogre comes out, sets his drum down and stands behind it).

"And now I will play my singing drum for you," said the ogre.
  He began to beat his drum…

(The ogre mimes beating the drum using large arm movements. Provide soft drumming sound effects.)

and Amanzi began to sing.

(The child who made the Amanzi puppet sings Amanzi's song through the cardboard tube from behind the curtain.)

She had heard voices which sounded like her parents, so she sang her favorite song—a song which described the beautiful sights around her village. She sang about the prancing striped zebras with their tails held high and the gazelles springing gracefully into space.

(If the children made Poster Board Rod Puppets [See "Variations"], they can hold them up from behind the curtain and move them along the top in the actions described. Hit together the open ends of two empty plastic yogurt containers for zebra hoofbeats. Twang a stringed instrument or hit a cymbal for the gazelle leaps.)

She sang about the gaily colored butterflies fluttering across the grassy plains before the distant purple mountains.

(If your group made Vibrant Butterfly Puppets, they can fly them out from behind one side of the curtain and flutter them across the entire width of the curtain. The puppeteers should flutter their puppets slowly across the stage in front of the masked performers to give the audience a clear view of their puppets. Then they can disappear behind the other side of the curtain. Wind chimes make a nice musical accompaniment.)

When Amanzi's parents heard the singing, they knew at once that it was their daughter's voice. Was that not her very own song? But they did not say a word.

(Amanzi's parents cover their mask mouths with their hands.)

"That's enough," bellowed the ogre. "I am too hungry to play anymore."

(The ogre throws up his arms, then rubs his belly.)

The villagers presented the ogre with their finest foods.

(The villagers present food to the ogre, who pretends to eat it.)

Amanzi's parents encouraged the ogre to eat more and more and to drink many calabashes of mealie beer.

(The parents pat the ogre on the shoulder and offer him more food and drink.)

Finally the ogre was so bloated with food and drink, he set his drum to one side and fell into a stuporous sleep.

(The ogre moves his drum to one side edge of the curtain. Then he falls over and begins to snore.)

The villagers returned to their huts to sleep.

(The villagers pick up their food baskets and disappear behind the curtain.)

When everyone was asleep, Amanzi's parents tiptoed over to peek inside the drum.

(The parents act out these movements.)

They were looking into the frightened eyes of their small daughter. They pulled her out and hugged her warmly. Then they took her to a safe place.

(The parents pull out the Amanzi puppet and hug her. Then they disappear behind the curtain and give the Amanzi puppet to her puppeteer. The mother picks up the container of paper thorns and the father locates his torch.)

Amanzi's mother dumped sharp acacia thorns into the drum.

(Amanzi's mother comes out and shakes the paper thorns out of the bowl and into the drum.)

Then Amanzi's father took a flaming branch from a campfire and used it to chase many wild bees from their hive in a dead tree. Amanzi's father herded the bees into the drum.

(Children with Buzzing Bee Puppets come out humming through their kazoos followed by Amanzi's father waving his torch in the air. The bees should come out from the side of the curtain which is opposite the drum. They can then buzz their way across the front of the curtain. When they get to the other side of the curtain, the children should *pretend* to fly their bees right into the drum—then they should duck behind the curtain with their bee puppets still in their hands. Additional sound effects can be added if the narrator also hums through a kazoo during the bee's flight.)

Then Amanzi's parents closed the drum tightly.

(Amanzi's parents close the drum and disappear behind the curtain.)

When the warm sun filled the sky,

(The Flamboyant Sun rises, accompanied by its sound effect.)

the villagers approached the big man.

(The villagers come out. The ogre wakes up and stretches.)

"Please play your wonderful drum for us one more time and we will give you a most delicious breakfast."

(The villagers make pleading gestures.)

"Alright," grumbled the ogre, "but I am too hungry to play more than one song."

(The ogre picks up his drum and sets it down next to the villagers, then he stands behind it.)

The ogre began to play his drum, thinking of the food which would soon be his—but, there was no singing!

(The ogre mimes beating the drum with big arm movements. No singing follows this time. The villagers put their hands to their ears, shrug and look at each other. Provide soft sound effects for drumbeats.)

The ogre was becoming angry. He beat the drum more forcefully.

(The ogre shakes his fist at the drum before beating it with larger and more determined arm gestures. Provide louder sound effects for the drum.)

Still there was no singing.
The villagers began to shake their heads and turn away from him.

(The villagers act out their parts.)

"All right, little girl," said the ogre, as he grabbed the drum and carried it away. "You will be my breakfast."

(The ogre picks up the drum and carries it over to the side edge of the curtain. There he turns it upside down, holds it high and shakes it angrily until the paper thorns fall out.)

Sharp thorns fell from the drum and lodged in his feet…

(The ogre drops the drum and hops up and down, holding first one foot, then the other.)

then the angry bees rushed out of the drum.

(The bee puppeteers come out from behind the curtain holding their bees low and making it look as if the bees are coming from the drum. They raise their kazoos to their mouths and begin buzzing through the kazoos—bees bobbing on top—as they chase the ogre. The chase should be portrayed in slow motion with the ogre lifting his knees high, swatting at his head and yowling in pain. The bees should follow him relentlessly, darting at his head from time to time. The group makes its way across the front of the curtain, moving around the outside of the group of villagers, and disappears around the other side of the curtain. The narrator can hum through a kazoo during the bees' flight to supplement the sound of angry bees.)

That ogre was never seen again.

(The parents and the child operating the Amanzi hand puppet come out in front of the curtain and gesture as if talking to the villagers.)

Amanzi and her parents waved to the villagers, then they began their long journey home.

(Everyone waves.)

They traveled for many days and nights.

(The Flamboyant Sun and Drifting Moon rise and fall several times in rapid succession from behind the curtain. Accompany each appearance with the proper sound effect. While this is happening, Amanzi and her parents walk around slowly in front of the curtain and the villagers disappear, still waving, behind the curtain.)

Then they saw the gleaming ocean in the distance, and they heard the gentle lowing of their village cattle…

(Everyone behind the curtain makes low mooing sounds.)

and they knew they were home again at last.

(Repeat musical theme, if you used one.)

And that ends our tale of the singing drum.
Sala kahle!

(*Sala kahle* is the Xhosa term for "good-bye." The entire cast comes out in front of the curtain and bows to the audience.)

Characters	What to Construct	Number
Amanzi	Hand-Mouth Puppet	1
elephant	1 Poster Board Animal Mask with cloth body*	2 children
lion	1 Saw-Toothed Lion Puppet	2 children
giraffe	1 giraffe puppet	2 children
ogre	Grocery Bag Mask	1
sun	Flamboyant Sun Scenery	1
moon	Drifting Moon Scenery	1
parents	Paper Plate Masks	2
villagers	Paper Plate Masks	3 to 10
bees	Buzzing Bee Puppet	3 to 10
butterflies (optional)	Vibrant Butterfly Puppet	3 to 10
stars (optional)	Singing Star Scenery	3 to 10
Zebra & Gazelle(optional)	Poster Board Rod Puppets**	3 to 10

*(See directions for converting this mask into a two-person puppet in the "Additional Props and Information" section that follows.)
**(You will find instructions for making Poster Board Rod Puppets in the "Variations" section that follows.)

Stages

To dramatize this story, use the Rope Curtain Stage, the Ladder Curtain Stage or the Freestanding Curtain Stage.

Group Scenery Projects

1. The children can decorate the curtain with scenes of grasslands, scattered trees and distant purple and blue mountains.

2. They can decorate a piece of blue cloth roughly 2' x 5' to look like the ocean. Waves and fish can be drawn on the cloth with felt-tip markers or oil pastels. Touches of glitter glue can portray sparkles of reflected sunlight.

3. Food can be drawn and cut out of construction paper: pumpkins, yams, red beans, bananas, bowls of porridge, chicken, gourds of goat's milk and mealie beer. Once it is made, this food can be distributed into baskets or wooden bowls, or make paper bowls by rolling down the top edges of brown paper grocery bags.

4. The children can make construction paper seashells for Amanzi to find. They can also decorate the drum.

Paper bags can be rolled down to form baskets filled with paper fruit and vegetables. Give children an opportunity to sculpt and paint papier-mâché food if time allows.

Additional Props and Information

• Keep the following considerations in mind for the child who is making the Amanzi puppet:

Before assigning roles in this dramatization ask for a volunteer who enjoys singing and isn't shy about singing in a loud, clear voice. Choose Amanzi from one of these volunteers.

Provide the child with a sheet of white poster board, a brown paper grocery bag and a pair of scissors in addition to the other materials for making a Hand-Mouth Puppet (See Chapter 2). After the Amanzi puppet's head has been designed and decorated and the garment-body attached, instruct the child to draw two legs with feet for Amanzi. These can then be cut out, colored with crayons and stapled to the front bottom edge of the puppet's garment. A shell-gathering bowl can be made by rolling the top of the grocery bag down until the bag resembles a shallow bowl with a rounded lip.

Keep a cardboard tube or a rolled sheet of paper behind the curtain. The child who made the Amanzi puppet will sing through this tube from behind the curtain whenever Amanzi is supposed to be singing from inside the drum.

The puppeteer who plays Amanzi can sing a simple tune when the story calls for it. A song from Africa—if the puppeteer knows one—would be great! If not, the child can make up a simple melody or chant which will be easily remembered. The lyrics can be simpli-

fied to "la la la" or "na na na," or whatever the child feels comfortable with.

• You can use a large empty tin for the ogre's drum. It has to be large enough to hold the Amanzi puppet, and it must have a lid which can be *easily* taken on and off by a child. You can make a flip lid from a circle of sturdy cardboard and attach it on one side of the tin with duct tape hinges.

You can also make a drum from three pieces of poster board. Put one sheet of poster board on top of another sheet, lining up the edges. Roll this double-thick poster board into a big cylinder, with a very small amount of overlap. Staple and tape the poster boards securely into this position, forming the body of the drum. Place the bottom of the cylinder on a third piece of poster board. Trace around the bottom of the cylinder. Now draw a circle about 1" larger around the traced circle. Cut this larger circle out. Cut a few slits around the edge reaching in to the smaller circle. Bend these tabs up. Set the cylinder into the circle, and glue and tape the tabs securely around the bottom, forming the bottom of the drum. Place the top end of the drum on the remaining section of poster board. Draw a circle on the poster board which is slightly larger than the top of the cylinder. Cut this circle out and place it on top of the drum. Use two hinges of tape or twine to attach the lid to the cylinder on one side—but allow the lid to be flipped back when the drum is opened. The poster board drum can be decorated with felt-

Use staples, tape, and twine or duct tape hinges to make a hollow drum prop out of poster board.

169

tip markers, tempera paints or water colors. Glue colorful geometric shapes made from construction or tissue paper to the sides of the tin drum.

• The child who makes the father Paper Plate Mask should also make a torch. Tape flame-colored cellophane or construction paper to one end of a cardboard tube, short stick or branch. The child making the mother Paper Plate Mask should cut several black or brown construction paper triangles to represent the thorns. These can be placed in a brown paper bag with its edges rolled down to form a bowl.

• Provide the child making the ogre Grocery Bag Mask with a piece of string or a pipe cleaner, scissors, tape and white poster board. Cut teeth out of the poster board, and attach them to the string to represent a leopard's-teeth bracelet. The ogre will look convincingly gluttonous if you use a sash to tie a pillow in front of the child's tummy and cover this artificial belly with a simple cloth toga-like costume (a section of brightly colored cloth knotted over one shoulder).

• The elephant can be made from a Poster Board Animal Mask and a piece of lightweight gray cloth draped over two puppeteers. If desired, construct four elephant legs to add to the puppet's bulk. Have the children use the side of a gray crayon or a gray oil pastel stick to add a coat of color to one side of four full-size pieces of white poster board. Add black wrinkle lines. Roll each piece of poster board into a wide cylinder—gray side out—and secure this shape with glue, paper fasteners or staples (a long-reach stapler is ideal for this job). The children can step into these legs before they shuffle out as the elephant.

Positioning

Drape the ocean cloth over a couple of chairs 2' or 3' away from one side of the curtain. Scatter the paper shells on the floor near the ocean.

The child with the Amanzi puppet comes out from behind the curtain on the ocean side. After the Amanzi puppet is put into the drum, this child can stand directly behind the curtain and sing through a cardboard tube.

The animals can wait behind the curtain, off to the side of the room, or just outside the door to the room.

The ogre can wait just behind the curtain or off to one side of the room. He makes his first appearance from the side opposite the ocean.

The sun and moon wait behind the curtain near the center and hold their scenery up from this position.

Amanzi's parents wait in some out-of-the-way spot or behind the curtain until they come out on the ocean side of the curtain.

The villagers wait in a tight group behind the curtain until they make their entrance from the side opposite the ocean. When they do appear, they stand as a group in front of the curtain and near this same side.

The bees, stars and butterflies can wait well behind the curtain.

The bowl of thorns and the torch should be placed in a safe place behind the curtain until it is time for the Amanzi's parents to use them.

Variations

• If your group is small, have the children who make and operate the bees also construct and operate the butterfly puppets. Also combine the sun and moon into one prop with the sun on one side and the moon on the other. This combo could be constructed and operated by one child.

• If you are working with a large group, some of the children can make and operate stars. Whenever the moon appears in the story narrative, insert an additional reference to the stars.

Another option for a large group is to have a few children draw and color gazelles and zebras on white poster board. These can be cut out and a T-shape control rod attached to each animal to form Poster Board Rod Puppets. When Amanzi sings about the beautiful sights she has seen, these puppets can appear to prance and leap along the top of the curtain.

• If construction time is short, have children make a Poster Board Animal Mask for the lion puppet. Instead of building the entire Stately Giraffe Puppet, draw a head and neck on sturdy cardboard. Cut it out and paint it. This shortcut puppet can poke its head and neck up from behind the curtain when it is time for the giraffe to appear.

• Use this project to provide papier-mâché sculpting opportunities for students. They can use this medium to add dimension to their masks and to sculpt more realistic food items.

Backstage view of Poster Board Rod Puppets leaping along the crossbar of a curtain.

TEN

Creating a Story from Scratch

Where Can We Find a Good Story for Twenty-Three Frog Puppets?

This book has offered suggestions for guiding a group of children through dramatizations of three international folktales. What steps do you take if your group wants to write an original story for dramatization?

There are probably as many ways to write a story as there are stories to write. This chapter describes a few methods which can help you organize such a project.

The first time you start out on a story-writing project with children, you may worry that nothing will happen. You might picture yourself staring at an empty piece of paper and a sea of blank faces. In reality, you will probably have trouble keeping up with the avalanche of ideas. Your main problem becomes that of any good organizer. While encouraging the free flow of ideas, you must help students form their story into a cohesive whole. There may be so many ideas that a fair method of reaching a decision, such as a group vote, must be employed.

If it becomes necessary for the group to vote on an aspect of the story, make sure children understand that any suggestions not chosen for this project remain valuable suggestions which could prove useful for creating a different story. But this story is a cooperative group project, and it is therefore only fair to have choices made by group vote. Remind students that each of them is free to write a story of his or her own design at any time.

Make sure you are prepared to record the story as it develops. Be equipped with a notebook and a couple of pencils or pens. When jotting down children's story ideas, leave a space between contributions so you will have room to insert new developments as the story progresses. If you have a large amount of blackboard space, you might use this to record their ideas.

Discussing Story Elements

When everyone is seated comfortably together, explain to the children that they are to become a writing team—a group working together to create an original story. There are endless possibilities, and their story will be more interesting if everyone helps by contributing suggestions and ideas. Use the story elements discussed below as your guides. Explain an element of the story (style, place, time, etc.), then solicit students' ideas by asking questions. Allow time for brainstorming at each stage of development. When you are ready to make a choice, arrive at a consensus by group vote. The children can then move on to the next step. The steps may overlap or supersede each other as the discussion progresses. You may choose to start at the bottom and work your way up; the creative process is not famous for orderliness. Just keep your pencil and paper handy to capture the cascade of suggestions.

Style: The group can decide what type of story to write. Will it be an origin story—a tale that explains why things are the way they are (*Why Fish Can't Sing*)? Will it be a fable—a story to teach a lesson (*The Tortoise and the Hare*)? Will it be a scary story—a story which gradually builds to a suspenseful climax and leaves its audience in a swirling pool of adrenaline (*The Legend of Sleepy Hollow*)? Will it be a fantasy—a tale of unrestrained imagination and whim (*Alice in Wonderland*)? Will it be an action-adventure story—in which its protagonist is confronted with a problem or a threat that must be dealt with (*The Singing Drum* and *The Ogre's Staircase*)? Or will it be a story which includes all these elements?

Place: Have the students discuss the locale of their story. Will the action take place on their own school playground or on another planet? Will the characters live in a distant country? A city? A desert? A rain forest? A drop of water? Or a fantasy world of their own invention? How would they describe this place to someone who had never seen it?

Time: During what period in time do students wish their story to occur? Will it be a tale from the past, the present or the future? Is the story to ring with the ancient clamor of armored knights, or will it float in the singing silence of a lonely space station?

Characters: Now that the setting has formed, it's time to shape the figures who will live there. Who are the characters in this story? Are they citizens of Saturn? Jungle animals? Sea creatures? Prehistoric giants? Microscopic beasties? Circus performers? Moonflower fairies?

Who are the protagonists (the heroes or heroines)? Who are the antagonists (villains)? What other characters are involved in this story?

Once the characters have been chosen, examine and develop their personalities. What is this character like? Is he young, lazy, clever, mischievous? Is she greedy, wise, energetic, brave? How do they act when they are frightened? What makes them happy? What are their dreams? What motivates their actions and behavior?

Plot: The plot usually consists of three main elements:

- *the initial action*

  How does the story start? What happens when these new and untried characters are placed in their carefully constructed world. How do they interact?

- *the conflict*

  What is the problem to be overcome? What is the challenge to be met? What is the mystery to be solved? How do the characters feel about it? What do they decide to do about it?

- *the resolution*

  Do the characters successfully deal with their problem? How are they changed? Is every character satisfied with the results? How does the story end?

Once the major decisions have been worked out by the group, it is up to you to put the story into a manageable form. If the story is going be dramatized, it will probably be most helpful if the story is told by a narrator. This serves a duel purpose during the performance of having the narrator giving cues to the performers while revealing the story's plot to the audience.

USING A FILL-IN-THE-BLANKS STORY OUTLINE

If a more structured method of story development appeals to you, try using the fill-in-the-blanks approach. Read the following story outline aloud, pausing at each blank space while the children work together to fill in the details. This story outline is designed to be developed into an action-adventure story.

Our story begins in

_____

(Decide on a time period for the story action.)

and takes place in/on

_____

(Fill in a story locale.)

a place of

_____

(Give a description of the locale.)

This was the home of

_____

(Fill in the name of the story's protagonist(s). The name Iggy will be used for this example just substitute the name your group chooses.)

Iggy was

_____

(Make up a physical description of your protagonist and describe some of his/her personality traits.)

It seemed to be just another day. Iggy ate breakfast with his/her family

(Fill in with a description of the protagonist's family.)

and spent some time with friends.

(Describe the protagonist's friends and what they did.)

But this day was to be different, for this was the day Iggy's troubles began.

(Describe the trouble. This may be a good topic for group brainstorming, with the final decision arrived at by group vote.)

Because of this problem, things changed for Iggy.

(Describe how the problem affects Iggy.)

Iggy's problem seemed insurmountable. What could Iggy do? Iggy's friends and family offered to help him/her think of a plan. Everyone made suggestions.

(Solicit suggestions from the group. The children can discuss which plan they feel would make the best story, then vote on the final plan.)

"I think I know what I must do," said Iggy. "Thanks for your help.

Tomorrow I will try my plan." Then Iggy went to sleep, heartened by the hope of finally solving the dilemma. Morning came....

(The arrivals of night and day offer good opportunities to use active scenery (stars, moon, sun, etc.) in a dramatization.)

and Iggy awoke feeling

(Describe Iggy's feelings.)

Iggy began to put his/her plan into effect.

(Describe any preparations Iggy would have to make.)

And then it happened.

(Describe the confrontation and climax.)

And from then on

(Describe any consequences or outcomes.)

And that is the end of our story.

Once the children have filled in the blanks to develop their version of the story, they can decide on a good name for it. You may want to tighten up the narration and polish any ragged edges so that it flows smoothly when read aloud, but tell the story in the children's own words and phrases whenever possible. The story is now written and ready to dramatize.

DRAMATIZING YOUR ORIGINAL STORY

Once the story is written, look through the chapters on puppets and masks to help you find suitable options for your story. Some characters may need to pick up or hold objects in their hands. Keep this in mind when deciding on a type of puppet or mask. You will probably find several options for each character. Using different types and sizes of storytelling aids in your dramatization can be very effective. And don't forget about the possibilities for using active scenery.

BUILDING A STORY AROUND A CAST OF CHARACTERS

Another approach to creating an original dramatization is to come up with some imaginary characters and let the story evolve from them. Provide children with all the materials needed to make a certain type of puppet or mask,

and let them develop these into any kind of imaginary character they wish. Once students have finished, they can take turns showing their creations to the other children. Encourage them to invent details about their created character and its personality. Ask a few questions to help in this process. Is the puppet or masked character friendly? Shy? Selfish? Greedy? Scary? Wise? Clumsy? Mysterious? What kinds of things does it like to do? Where does it live? What frightens it? What are its talents?

Once the characters have been developed, suggest that the children think about how these characters might interact if they met each other. You could all work together using the story-writing elements suggested previously to develop a story which uses all their creations. Or you might prefer to assign children to smaller groups and ask each group to develop its own story using their creations as the main characters.

Once you begin to offer opportunities for children to use their artistic creations for dramatic storytelling, you will begin to think of other ways these elements can be combined and utilized. You will discover new teaching techniques, and your students will discover a satisfying outlet for their creative abilities. Enjoy yourselves!

INDEX

Notes

Notes